The rainforest is worth saving and, in fact, must be saved. Michael Pink has the most brilliant and original way to do it: get make-it-happen wealth builders and businesspeople to start thinking of these ideas and models and being inspired to these exciting mind-set changing and improving ideas. We will get rich and save the environments simultaneously.

MARK VICTOR HANSEN
Coauthor, *Chicken Soup for the Soul* and *The One Minute Millionaire*

Michael Pink has a gift for seeing universal truths in the world around us and translating them into the business world with eye-opening clarity and practical relevance. The truths in this book will transform your business. The strategies and action steps Pink includes offer the chance to convert sometimes ephemeral truths into concrete actions that are duty-bound to take your business to the next level.

ROD THOMSON
Executive Editor, *Gulf Coast Business Review*

In over a decade and a half of friendship with Michael Pink, I have repeatedly seen him turn timeless truths into practical takeaways for life and leadership—and now he has done it again—this time through a remarkable and revealing journey through the rainforest. Throughout this book you will find the soil of your heart and mind being seeded with fresh insights and perspectives as Michael unearths the seven secrets hidden within it. This is truly a great resource for business beginners, a hands-on encouragement for those growing their companies, and an outstanding tool for marketplace mentors.

DAVE BUEHRING
Founder and Team Leader, Lionshare Leadership Group

Groundbreaking! Michael Pink has delivered a top-notch blueprint for any CEO or entrepreneur who wants to take their business to new levels. *Rainforest Strategy* will transform not only the way you approach business but also the way you live!

TIM P. ROGERS
President, Rogers Promotional Marketing

This is the most powerful business book that I have ever read. I will make it required reading for the senior executives in our firms. Thanks, Michael Pink, for doing the research to share these valuable insights with us.

KENT HUMPHREYS
410 Investments

Michael Pink gives all of us a lot to learn and apply in his interesting new book. I know you'll be as fascinated with his insights and conclusions as I was.

PAT WILLIAMS
Senior Vice President, Orlando Magic
Author, *The Pursuit*

I would like to commend Michael Pink for his unique approach and insight into business. In this book, he teaches us the lessons of nature, whereby we can learn the biggest secrets of wealth building. I strongly recommend this book to all, as it is a new approach, a new understanding, and fresh insight into this sphere of life. I believe that it will be a blessing to all who read it.

SUNDAY ADELAJA
Senior Pastor and Founder
The Embassy of the Blessed Kingdom of God for All Nations
Kiev, Ukraine

What does a rainforest have to do with success in business? Plenty, according to my friend Michael Pink in his book, *Rainforest Strategy*. It's not surprising we can gain valuable insights to succeed in business from nature. However, it requires someone to help us extract and understand these secrets in hidden places. (See Isaiah 45:3.) Michael reveals hundreds of valuable business principles revealed in nature that you can apply to succeed in business and life. If you're looking for an edge, you'll gain many valuable tools here. I highly recommend this groundbreaking book.

OS HILLMAN
Author, *The 9 to 5 Window* and *TGIF: Today God Is First*

Michael Pink has raised the bar! This book will help you do twice as much in half the time…with a lot less stress. These rapid-growth business strategies adapted from the rainforest are simply brilliant!

PETER LOWE
Get Motivated Seminars

Tropical rainforests are known as the jewels of the earth, and from this rich environment Michael Pink has unearthed seven wealth secrets that will enrich your life. This captivating study is nothing short of inspired. You will get far more out of your life, job, and business if you tap into the dynamic principles so powerfully communicated in this book.

TAMARA LOWE
Get Motivated Seminars

I have greatly enjoyed reading Michael Pink's new book, *Rainforest Strategy*. It will have an impact on anyone in business—particularly those in leadership positions.

The rainforest model for the book is intriguing. Michael has included so much biological and scientific information—it is bound to grasp the interest of any reader, particularly how each event in the rainforest relates to and illustrates a business principle.

The techniques Michael outlines will help make any product successful and should even be considered during the development process. Irresistible!

WES CANTRELL
Former CEO of Lanier

Rainforest
STRATEGY

Rainforest
STRATEGY

MICHAEL Q. PINK

EXcel
BOOKS
A STRANG COMPANY

Most STRANG COMMUNICATIONS/CHARISMA HOUSE/CHRISTIAN LIFE/ EXCEL BOOKS/FRONTLINE/REALMS/SILOAM products are available at special quantity discounts for bulk purchase for sales promotions, premiums, fund-raising, and educational needs. For details, write Strang Communications/Charisma House/Christian Life/Excel Books/ FrontLine/Realms/Siloam, 600 Rinehart Road, Lake Mary, Florida 32746, or telephone (407) 333-0600.

RAINFOREST STRATEGY by Michael Q. Pink
Published by Excel Books
A Strang Company
600 Rinehart Road
Lake Mary, Florida 32746
www.strangdirect.com

Scripture quotations marked KJ21 are from the 21st Century King James Version, copyright © 1994 by Deuel Enterprises, Inc. Used by permission.

Scripture quotations marked NKJV are from the New King James Version of the Bible. Copyright © 1979, 1980, 1982 by Thomas Nelson, Inc., publishers. Used by permission.

Design Director: Bill Johnson
Cover Designer: Karen Grindley, Bill Johnson

Library of Congress Cataloging-in-Publication Data:
An application to register this book for cataloging has been filed with
the Library of Congress.
International Standard Book Number: 978-1-59979-372-6

First Edition

08 09 10 11 12 — 987654321
Printed in the United States of America

DEDICATION

FOR BRENDA

I told you when we got married we would go places, but neither of us knew where that promise would take us. You have traveled with me to some far-flung places when staying at home would have been much easier on you.

You have stuck by me through culture shock and climate shock. You have pressed on when most would have turned back. You have been bitten by just about any insect that flies and some that don't. When you said, "for better or worse," you really meant it!

You were the first to read this book, proofing it for typos, checking it for accuracy, and giving countless helpful suggestions along the way that are now part of this book. People will think me really smart, but we both know a lot of the good stuff came from you!

You are simply an unbelievably courageous, generous, and kindhearted person who happens to be my very best friend and the love of my life.

You are *pura vida* to me, my Berachah!

ACKNOWLEDGMENTS

I WANT TO THANK JOSEPH AND LINDSAY JOHNSON FOR THEIR gracious hospitality and for allowing their company to be a laboratory for testing all of the rainforest principles and implementing them faithfully. More than that, I am grateful, Joe, for our working partnership and friendship that defy the ordinary. Whether racing me up the steep incline of a Mayan temple in a sweltering jungle or crossing a dubious-looking river barefoot in Belize, you have shown yourself to be a true friend, closer than a brother.

I want to acknowledge Cheryl Clunk, our office administrator who holds things together for us while we are traveling to every corner of the earth. Her undying loyalty and friendship have meant the world to us! Jill Johnson (no relation to Joseph) provided valuable research assistance for the book at all hours while her husband (my good friend), David, worked tirelessly to implement many of our findings into our business model. He once introduced me as a speaker at one of his Nourish the Dream events by saying that I was known for Selling Among Wolves, but I would be remembered for my work on the rainforest! Mark Herron, my lifelong graphic artist, cheered me on throughout the writing of this book and helped me greatly in the early stages to formulate and crystallize the concepts and wording of the wealth secrets contained herein.

Frank Morrice Arias and Frank Morrice Jimenez, owners of Century 21 Semusa Realty in Panama City, Panama, gave generously of their time, making valuable introductions in Panama and making our time there more productive. I want to thank the highly talented team at Strang Communications for recognizing the potential of this book and being such a pleasure to work with. And lastly but most importantly, I want to acknowledge in all my ways the One who made the rainforest in the first place and disclosed a few of its secrets to me.

CONTENTS

Foreword *by Zig Ziglar*..xv

Introduction 1

Chapter 1: The Epiphany
Better Than Gold...3

Chapter 2: Breaking the Code
The Mystery Unfolds.. 13

Chapter 3: Spontaneous Wealth
Seeing What Others Miss... 23

Chapter 4: Wealth Secret #1: The Fungus Factor
Getting the Most From the Least............................... 39

Chapter 5: Practice Abundance
Or Experience Scarcity.. 67

Chapter 6: Wealth Secret #2: Grow Toward the Light
Powered by Vision..89

Chapter 7: Wealth Secret #3: Enter the "No Pest Zone"
7 Natural Laws to Get Control of Your Time............ 113

Chapter 8: The Pathogen Problem
Defeating What's Been Eating You 137

Chapter 9: Wealth Secret #4: The Photosynthesis of Ideas
Turning Vision Into Provision 151

Chapter 10: Wealth Secret #5: The Strangler Fig Phenomenon
A Lesson in Timing.. 167

Chapter 11: Wealth Secret #6: The Brazil Nut Effect
Leverage Through Strategic Relationships............... 185

Chapter 12: Wealth Secret #7: The Orchid Element
Creating Irresistibility 197

Conclusion... 219

Notes 221

FOREWORD

T'S NOT OFTEN I HAVE THE OPPORTUNITY TO LEARN SOMETHING totally new to me. Much of what I have been teaching for nearly fifty years had been said before, has been said many times since, and will undoubtedly be said over and over again as years come and go. The bottom line is success principles do not change. They were given to us originally in God's Word, and they work regardless of whether we credit them to God or not.

Michael Pink's adaptation of the truths of the rainforest to success in business is unique and fascinating. I was unprepared for how intricately woven these principles are. The message in this book reawakened me to just how exciting and eye-opening new applications of old values can be. His understanding of the rainforest and its application to structuring and conducting business in today's world makes for interesting and thought-provoking reading. *Rainforest Strategy* reveals simultaneously remarkable facts about the rainforest and effective leadership skills. It offers good insight along with practical, workable suggestions, policies, and processes. The procedures it recommends can be applied to virtually any business of any size and purpose, and Michael shares plenty of specific "how-tos" for easing transitions.

I believe business leaders at all levels can benefit from the information in this book. Michael's writing style keeps your attention and piques your interest as he shares what he has learned without reverting to textbook tedium. I am of the opinion that the information in *Rainforest Strategy* can be a positive factor in your future and the future of your business.

ZIG ZIGLAR

INTRODUCTION

YOU HOLD IN YOUR HAND A BOOK WITH INVALUABLE INFORMA-tion that can revolutionize your life and your business. It took me three years of study from both rare and common sources to acquire this specialized knowledge, not to mention the firsthand lessons gleaned from exploring the rainforests of Belize, Panama, Costa Rica, Tobago, and British Columbia. The investment of time and treasure was sizeable but pales in comparison to the value I have received from my study.

I write it here in this book as much for your benefit as for mine. You see, it was in pulling the years of research together that I got so much value from it. It helped me get the message deep on the inside and guaranteed me the highest benefit. Try writing a book sometime, and you will see just how much you learn in the process! The downside for you getting it in this form is that we tend to esteem lightly what costs us little. Because the knowledge in this book cost me so much person-ally, I am getting much from it. You will have to be very deliberate about applying the truths herein to gain similar value.

We all see through a glass darkly, here a little, there a little, each of us with a piece. It is my hope that the piece I bring to the table with this book will complement the many pieces you have already acquired throughout your life. One of my struggles in writing it was knowing I would learn so much more after writing it that I would want to include, but it would be too late.

To solve that problem and to give you the most value, consider joining us on a business excursion to a rainforest resort where we can observe firsthand the things written about in this book and discover many more besides. It's a time not only for discovery, but also for networking with like-minded business leaders with similar challenges as you come together to find workable solutions.

I have found a place with first-class accommodations, world-class executive meeting rooms, and access to the best guides on the planet—all in a tropical rainforest setting that is just a few hours by plane from Texas or Florida. Check it out at www.GamboaResort.com.

In the meantime, and to get you in the mood, get you a big cup of dark roasted, Central American, organically grown, fresh-brewed coffee, find your favorite place to read, and get ready for a treat! You are about to enter *the rainforest zone...*

1

THE EPIPHANY
Better Than Gold

Gratitude bestows reverence, allowing us to encounter
everyday epiphanies, those transcendent moments of awe
that change forever how we experience life and the world.[1]

JOHN MILTON

EVERYTHING YOU NEED TO LEARN ABOUT BUSINESS CAN BE *learned in the rainforest.* Those words landed on my soul like distant thunder with an authority only a father can bring, yet I was alone. They were at once reassuring and at the same time seemingly preposterous. How could anyone learn anything about business from observing an ecosystem as yet untouched by man? My own question contained the seeds of the answer. It was a system, an "eco" system.

The night before that thunderous idea hit my soul, my wife and I were enjoying some fresh seviche, a local favorite consisting of tropical fish marinated in citrus and served with lightly salted chips that made our arduous journey to the mountain village of Boquete, Panama, well worth the effort. It's a top retirement choice for many Americans due to its eternal springlike climate where temperatures seldom get above the mid-eighties by day or below the mid-fifties by night. The air was thick with the fragrance of orchids, and the sounds of exotic birds enchanted our every moment.

As we dined in an open-air café under the slowly turning ceiling fan, watching the sun kiss the mountains good night, I overheard two women discussing their travel that day into the rainforest. Their voices were filled with wonder and utter amazement at what they had seen. They described another world, a world I had never seen. It was Jurassic Park but not as dangerous. I knew I had to see it as soon as possible. It wasn't their description of beauty and exotic life-forms that grabbed my attention, but rather it was their observation of cooperation and relationship between species that piqued my interest.

They spoke in hushed, reverential tones about the symbiotic relationships between various insect species and how when you get about 100 feet inside the forest, you are enveloped by peace and quickly lose track of not only your sense of time, but also, as I later discovered, of every worry, concern, and stress that so easily plague us in our day-to-day lives. I was hooked! I had to get to the rainforest and experience this for myself. For that to occur, we would have to return, as our time there had come to an end.

Upon returning home, one of the first things I did was look on the Internet to see if anyone else had ever considered the notion of the rainforest as a business model. Immediately I found, *What We Learned in the Rainforest: Business Lessons from Nature* by Tachi Kiuchi, chairman and CEO Emeritus of Mitsubishi Electric America, and Bill Shireman, chairman and CEO of the Future 500. These guys had parachuted into Costa Rica and other rainforests, and what they observed changed the way they ran their businesses. They maintain that "by gleaning information from nature—the very system it once sought to conquer—business can learn how to adapt rapidly to changing market conditions and attain greater and more sustainable profits."[2] Wow! Maybe that thunderous thought I heard in Panama wasn't so far-fetched after all! Maybe the answers to my business challenges could be found in the rainforest.

Like many of you, I wanted to know how to survive and even thrive in the junglelike environment we compete in every day. I wanted to know how to succeed using the most time-proven principles of all, the principles built into nature itself. And like many of you, I was constrained by lack of resources. My vision outstripped provision, and I needed to find a solution.

ECO-SYSTEM...ECO-LOGIC...ECO-NOMICS

Interestingly enough, the word *ecosystem* is derived from the words *oikos* (which is Greek and means the home or household) and *system* (which is a set of interacting or interdependent entities forming an integrated whole). In other words, an ecosystem is a model of a complex system with multiple components executing varied processes to achieve a unified purpose. That sounds like business to me! In one very real sense, the rainforest is a business. It manufactures pure, breathable air for everyone on the planet to enjoy. Acting like lungs, the rainforest converts vast quantities of carbon dioxide (a poisonous gas that mammals exhale) into cool, refreshing, life-sustaining air through the process of photosynthesis.

In the rainforest, energy flows through various levels, ensuring the transformation of materials from one state to another. It begins with nonliving matter like gas, water, or minerals and turns them into living tissue in the form of plants. These are consumed by animals producing more tissue and ultimately waste as it's recycled through the system over and over again, teaching us among other things a great deal about efficiency. Just studying the processes that make this possible can revolutionize manufacturing alone, as Kiuchi and Shireman attest.

The word *economics* combines the Greek word *oikos* (household) with *nomos* (custom or law) to give us "the rules (or laws) of household management." Ecology goes one step further by studying the science, the "logic," the source code if you will, of what makes household management really work. When we look at economics, we explore the relationship between supply and demand, between producers and consumers, between spending and earning, between giving and receiving and what people can do to maximize their goals within that framework. The rainforest provides an excellent model for observation of these relationships.

What's interesting about ecology is that it goes beyond observing laws and interactions to arrive at the discovery of ways or principles that transcend time and place and can be applied anywhere. It's more than rules. It gives life and animates whatever is touched by it, be that business or family or government. When we study ecology, we peer into a higher form of learning, complex yet simple, dynamic and at the same time constant, and lush with principles, models, and even strategies waiting to be discovered. It gives us a glimpse into the mind of infinite wisdom, expressed in a myriad of ways through the things that are created.

Ecology and economies happen within a context—the context of community. Those communities or systems may well be a forest or mangrove, a coral reef or a family, a village, or even a city or business. When we approach the rainforest, we do so knowing it could represent any number of other communities from business to government to social circles. For the purpose of this book, we will look at the rainforest with entrepreneurial eyes to glean principles and strategies to help us succeed in business while at the same time getting in touch with the wisdom behind the systems. While I believe the rainforest is a picture of an economic system as a whole, I will focus on the specific truths that can turn companies into thriving enterprises while giving us all a greater sense of accomplishment in a context of more peace and greater meaning.

HIDDEN WEALTH

For centuries explorers have hacked their way through the jungles in search of gold, unaware they were surrounded by something better than gold if they only had eyes to see. There is so much information, so much revelation waiting to be harvested by studying the created order and, in particular, the highly abundant, lush rainforests found in tropical regions around the world. In recent years scientists have begun exploring the rainforest in search of cures for all manner of diseases—and with much success too. They have begun to recognize some of the wealth hidden in the primitive rainforests the world over. Companies like MonaVie and XanGo have turned to the rainforest to find exotic blends of natural berries full of powerful antioxidants to increase vitality and enhance life.

But there's more, much more. As we move beyond the industrial economy to a more knowledge-based economy, business is beginning to recognize that the real profit to be earned from nature comes from the principles by which it flourishes, more than the exploitation of its resources. The rainforest is the most fruitful, productive, and diverse ecosystem on the planet despite having limited capital. (It has limited, poor-quality topsoil.) So the question beckons: How does the rainforest deliver so much fruitfulness, so much productivity, and so much diversity from relative scarcity? The answer to this question is what every business owner, entrepreneur, and household manager needs to know, and I intend to show you!

By rightly discerning what makes the rainforest so fruitful and productive despite having to work with limited resources, and by wisely interpreting the systems of the rainforest, we can begin to assemble a model for business that has tremendous potential to revolutionize our businesses and our lives. Indeed, the way forward in business and life is to become more like a complex living system that adapts to change, conserves resources, and produces abundance—all without breaking a sweat!

Consider this: The Royal Library of Alexandria in Alexandria, Egypt, founded in 283 B.C. by Ptolemy II, was once the largest library in the world. It had over half a million documents from the ancient world, including Assyria, Greece, Persia, Egypt, India, and many other nations. Over one hundred scholars were said to have lived on-site working full-time to perform research, write, lecture, or translate and copy documents. This incredible treasure trove of ancient knowledge was burned to the ground in 48 B.C., with Julius Caesar being the most likely culprit. It has been considered the greatest loss of knowledge in history, but now, every day a greater source of knowledge is being destroyed in a misguided quest for gain.

ASTONISHING FACTS

According to the organization Save the Rainforest, "A typical four-mile square mile patch of rainforest contains as many as 1,500 species of flowering plants, 750 species of trees, 125 mammal species, 400 species of birds, 100 species of reptiles, 60 species of amphibians, and 150 different species of butterflies." They point out, "There are more fish species in the Amazon river system than in the entire Atlantic Ocean." And, "A single rainforest reserve in Peru is home to more species of birds than the entire United States."[3]

Here are some more facts from their site:

- At least 1,650 rainforest plants can be utilized as alternatives to our present fruit and vegetable staples.

- Thirty-seven percent of all medicines prescribed in the US have active ingredients derived from rainforest plants.

- Seventy percent of the plant species identified by the US National Cancer Institute as holding anti-cancer properties come from rainforests.

- Ninety percent of the rainforest plants used by Amazonian Indians as medicines have not been examined by modern science.

- Of the few rainforest plant species that have been studied by modern medicine, treatments have been found for childhood leukemia, breast cancer, high blood pressure, asthma, and scores of other illnesses.[4]

I am not a tree hugger by nature, but I have come to understand the importance of the ecosystems that sustain us and the responsibility we have to sustain them. With stunning disregard to our own mutual welfare, we have destroyed nearly half of the world's rainforests and, with them, most of the indigenous peoples dwelling therein. In Brazil alone, just five hundred years ago, there were up to ten million indigenous people living in the rainforest. Today, there are fewer than two hundred thousand left alive. We have increased nature's normal extinction rate by an estimated 10,000 percent, mostly in the rainforest where thousands of species are becoming extinct every year. Our corporate disregard of the natural order is currently causing the largest mass extinction since the dinosaur age, but at a much faster rate. We need to wake up!

Tropical rainforests circle the equator, maintaining a surprisingly cool, but comfortably warm temperature of roughly 80 degrees, with rainfall ranging from 160 to 400 inches per year, depending on location and terrain. Untouched by previous ice ages and maintaining constant warmth and water intake, tropical rainforests are home to an estimated sixty to eighty million different life-forms. Talk about diversity! But here's the dirty little secret that people like the Rainforest Action Network want us to know—more than an acre and a half of rainforest is lost every second. That's like burning an area more than twice the size of Florida every year![5] I hope we figure it out before we cut it all down and lose not only a critical life-sustaining natural resource, but also all the wisdom that could have helped us going forward.

WISDOM FOUND

Speaking of wisdom, did you know that Solomon, the wisest man in history, had a passion to study and learn from the created order? According to Hebrew Scripture, Solomon "spoke of trees, from the cedar tree that is in Lebanon even unto the hyssop that springeth out of the wall. He spoke also of beasts, and of fowl, and of creeping things, and of fishes. And there came of all people to hear the wisdom of Solomon, from all kings of the earth, who had heard of his wisdom."[6] What is interesting is that Solomon let them determine the fee to be paid him for his wisdom. In one year alone, the weight of gold that came to him "was six hundred threescore and six talents."[7] (That's over $1 billion in today's money at current gold prices.) Besides that, he received revenue from the "merchants, and from the traffic of the spice merchants, and from all the kings of Arabia, and from the governors of the country."[8] In short, he was a very prosperous man.

Now, do you think the kings of the earth came to Solomon to learn how to prune an apple tree? Or is it possible that Solomon understood, like other towering figures of history, that the invisible traits of the unseen God are clearly seen by the things He has made?[9] That the wisdom of God can be learned in part by studying and reverse engineering the creation around us? That the created order is a textbook without pages containing more wisdom than we can uncover in a million lifetimes?

Come with me on this journey and discover, as Bill Shireman, president and CEO of Future 500, said in a 2002 keynote address to World Futures Society, "Yet despite this scarcity—or because of it—the rainforest is the MOST EFFECTIVE value-creating system in the world."

He wasn't the first to see it, nor the last. Thankfully, more and more business executives are waking to this truth. In the process, two things occur: First, we begin to value, then preserve, the rainforest as both a repository of wisdom and a storehouse of renewable, replenishable food and medicine with remarkable curative properties. Secondly, we begin to apply the lessons we learn from the rainforest and build enterprises that are self-generating, self-replicating centers of profit that provide immense value and harm none.

Since my first trip to the rainforest, I have been back to Panama a number of times. I have also explored the rainforests of Belize, Costa Rica, Tobago, and even Vancouver Island in British Columbia. The things I learned, we began to immediately apply. In fact, as noted on our Web site www.secretsoftherainforest.com, "Within 90 days of applying these principles, we tripled our staff, tripled our office size and I'm too embarrassed to tell you what happened to our revenues!" What I will tell you is that what used to be monthly revenues in our Internet business are now done (as of the writing of this chapter) a couple of times a day!

You will discover as you read this book what it means to be "rainforest compliant." It's a business term I have coined referring to businesses that purposefully employ business lessons from the rainforest. They are businesses that, where possible and feasible, mold and conform their practices, strategies, and operating principles to those observable in the rainforest and reap substantial, measurable, and lasting profit. As part of a larger study, I am currently working with a nonprofit entity to raise funds for a new breed of business school called the Spire School of Business. They have a global mission and require a substantial endowment to get started.

The foundation charged with raising the endowment for the school retained me to set up the structure and systems to achieve their endowment goals. My first order of business was to make them a working model of a "rainforest compliant" business and study the impact on revenues and profits. Prior to my involvement, in their first few years of existence, they had built an endowment of approximately $10 million. Since deliberately applying specific rainforest principles to their endowment growth, that amount has quintupled in only seven months to over $50 million.

If these principles and practical strategies adapted from the rainforest can actually help a former sales trainer (yours truly—www.SellingAmong Wolves.com) and business consultant turn a struggling Internet business into a thriving economic engine and help add $40 million in value to a previously unheard of nonprofit endowment in a matter of months, then you might want to consider taking a really close look at what follows in the subsequent chapters. Even if you think you know some of the subject matter, take the time to process the information and see it again in a fresh light.

I expect when you are finished reading this book, you will have had a few "Aha!" moments. Make sure to write down any ingenious ideas you get right away. Don't expect to remember them later. You won't. When you read this book, have a notepad with you to jot down ways you can apply the lessons to your business enterprises. When I travel in the rainforest, I carry a pen and pocket-sized notebook so I will be sure to capture the inspirations that seem to hang off every tree like ripe fruit just waiting to be picked. If you would like to join one of our rainforest expeditions where we explore the rainforest in the morning, then return to an upscale hotel near the rainforest to process what we just saw and discuss how to apply those lessons to revolutionize your business, then contact us at 877. 254.3047 or through www.RainforestStrategy.com.

I invested $50,000 to learn growth and management strategies in the rainforest just so I could improve my business. Although I received many times that investment back in short order, I also received the bonus of less stress going forward. On future rainforest quests, we plan to have proven business leaders who have successfully applied rainforest principles to their business pass on their wisdom in a classroom setting back at the rainforest hotel, and help us all grow strong and thriving businesses. The education won't be cheap, but ignorance is far more costly!

Step into the rainforest with me, and explore the unsearchable riches of wisdom safely embedded in all things living. Business fads come and go, but the wisdom in these pages has been around for a very long time and will not cease to be relevant in the future. Ignore at your own peril and proceed at your own risk, because it takes guts to act on what you are about to read. But if you act, even if you fail, you will learn invaluable life lessons that will serve you well in the future. The rainforest is a blueprint for success, but the execution is up to you, and poor execution, even with superb plans, can still result in failure.

Everyone wants to know the key to the incredible growth and productivity of the rainforest. Many assume it must be the rain. After all, it's a rainforest. Others assume the topsoil must be rich and plentiful, but it's not. Still others attribute it to the warmth of the tropical region or abundant sunlight. While it's true that warmth and light and water play an important role, they are, in fact, supporting roles for something so powerful the rainforest would be sparse without it. It is so subtle it is easily missed or ignored. It is so amazing that when you understand the significance of what it is and how it works, your business will never be the same again. I call it the fungus factor. But to understand it, you must first break the rainforest code.

BREAKING THE CODE
The Mystery Unfolds

The ignorant man marvels at the exceptional; the wise
man marvels at the common; the greatest wonder of all is
the regularity of nature.[1]

GEORGE D. BOARDMAN

Knowledge is of no value unless you put it into practice.[2]

ANTON CHEKHOV

HE RAINFOREST HAS ITS OWN LANGUAGE, ITS OWN RHYTHM, ITS
own mystery, just waiting to be discovered by those who care
enough to unravel it. For thousands of years, the indigenous
people of tropical rainforests lived by its rhythm, basked in its beauty,
dined from its bounty, and were healed by its many remedies. Now
today, we are taking another look at the rainforest from a more global
perspective. We will interpret the message or lessons of the rainforest
by observing the purpose a particular thing serves and the principles by
which it operates. For example, we ask, What role does light play? What,
in business, plays that same role or serves a similar purpose? What are
the principles governing the role of light in the rainforest? When you
understand the purpose and principles, you are well on your way to
interpreting the wisdom behind the systems that make the rainforest
so incredibly rich. What unfolds from this panorama of vibrant life and
endless abundance is something far less happenstance than you might
imagine. What emerges out of the apparent chaos is order.

For me, the most exciting discovery was not the matchless beauty and surprising comfort of the rainforest. It was the realization that the rainforest was an enterprise of sorts. It has functioned by nonnegotiable rules, producing consistent results for eons. These rules can be observed, measured, copied, and applied to other areas of life. They are free from corruption and nefarious influences that would bend the rules to support hidden agendas. They are pure, simple, and effective. They exist for their own purpose, but serve to instruct us if we will but have the perspective of an eagle, the curiosity of a child, and a heart of humility.

The rainforest is full of metaphors, business models, useful analogies, and observable trends, patterns, and relationships that mirror good business practices. You will learn how the rainforest economy runs without money, works interdependently, and creates abundance while maintaining an overwhelming sense of peace. The Smithsonian white papers I studied frequently during my research referenced business terms like *cost accounting* and the like when describing the way plants apportion resources to various roles. It seems to me that while none of us have the whole picture, the correlation between productivity in the rainforest and business was inescapable to the scientists who measure growth rates, resource consumption, and competition in the rainforest.

COLOR IS EXPENSIVE!

During my visit to Barro Colorado, an island in the Panama Canal, the Smithsonian scientist taking us through the rainforest remarked unexpectedly, "In the rainforest, color is very expensive." If she had said, "Color is very beautiful or eye-catching or diverse," I wouldn't have thought much of it, but she said color was "expensive." She went on to explain that color is used to attract "customers" such as birds or bees or other patrons to their tree to partake of their offer and in the process cause pollination to occur. She said that some trees actually drop all their leaves to conserve energy and then focus their remaining energy and attention on producing flowers to attract customers. She called that "marketing." The extent to which rainforest trees will go to market their wares is remarkable. It is so important that they are willing to shut down all other production and divert scarce resources into sales and marketing. If they are successful, they will produce even more fruit the following year. I thought I was there for a nature tour, and instead I found myself at the receiving end of a business lesson.

About twenty years ago in a period of lack, I had taken a walk in the woods to clear my head and find some solutions. I began thinking about the process of turning intangible ideas into tangible realities. Out of the blue, standing in front of a tall cedar tree, the thought penetrated my heart, "Where did the tree get its wood?" Did little chips of wood crawl through the forest at night and mass together little by little in the form of a tree? I knew where we got metal. We just dug it out of the ground. I knew where water and dirt came from, but I had no idea where wood came from. It just grew. Somehow I knew that when I found out where the tree got its wood, I would understand how to transform the intangible into tangible, spendable form.

I immediately left the woods, got in my car, and headed to the library to learn exactly what it took to transform a seed into a tree. I read about one eighteenth-century study that greatly impacted me. The study went something like this: A five-pound seedling was planted in a pot with twenty pounds of soil and placed in a room where it was watered and had plenty of light. Five years later, the seedling had gained ninety-five pounds of wood, but the soil had only lost an ounce of weight. Where did the wood come from? As it turned out, there were seven things that are always required to turn a seed into a tree. They are the seed, the soil, nutrients, water, light, warmth, and carbon dioxide (CO_2). As you will see shortly, the role they play when understood in business terms is highly relevant, totally practical, and very productive.

Modern scientists attribute the entire process to something called photosynthesis, but they readily admit they don't fully understand what really happens during this process. They can observe and measure WHAT happens and WHEN, but they haven't fully grasped the WHY quite yet, other than to say that light energy acts upon chlorophyll to convert air and water into glucose (food). What I'm going to do for you now is define the seven essential elements of seed, soil, water, light, and so on by their role and, with a little common sense or deductive logic, make a case for how you can interpret so much of what you see in nature into a language you speak and understand and live every day. While I am comfortable with the translation that follows, for other applications, other translations may apply.

1 **SEED—the idea.** This is the concept of your product or service. Purpose is known. Plans are in place, and you're ready to push through the surface into the light. It is fully actionable and ready to plant (invest resources in).

2 **SOIL—the initial investment or starting capital.** This is the seed money to feed the seed and get you launched. You can do surprisingly well with limited capital if you have all the other elements in place. Money is just time in folded form. The more you have, the more time you can save getting launched; however, if you are starting your first business, you may be better off with less cash. Here's why. Consider the butterfly. It must struggle to break out of its cocoon so it can have the strength to fly. If you assist it by peeling back the cocoon, it won't gain the strength to fly and it will die. Similarly, when you start a business, there is much to be learned in the struggle of the startup that equips you for success. Lots of cash can cut that short, but unless you are already a seasoned entrepreneur, the extra cash will only hide your deficiencies, leaving you vulnerable when lean times come.

3 **NUTRIENTS—a continuing supply of cash flow supporting the growth of the seed.** This comes from the process of exchanging one form of value for another, that is, the sale of your product, service, or ideas for cash. Cash flow or income can come from a variety of creative sources, including recycling waste or

repurposing old versions of a product or service into a new form or venue. Debt also provides cash, but unlike a nutrient that supports the seed, it acts like a toxin and drains the life from the seed. You can live with some toxins, but too much will kill the business. When your outgo exceeds your income, your upkeep will become your downfall.

4 **WATER—information.** There must be sufficient information and "know-how" so the participants in the venture know what to do and what direction they are heading. Throughout ancient literature, water is representative of information. It fuels growth. Think of it as communication. When communication or the flow of information is shut off, the business withers. Keep good communication channels open at all times so information and corporate know-how can flow through the enterprise. Always confirm the veracity of the information upon which you are making decisions. The bigger the decision, the more important to confirm the facts from multiple sources and in greater detail.

5 **LIGHT—vision.** As discussed in greater detail later, light enables vision, and vision is what drives the company. This is not the idea or seed. It's what *can become of the idea* and how it will affect everyone involved. It's the picture of the dream fully activated. The amount of light (vision) you have will directly determine the size and success of your enterprise. James Allen wisely said, "You will become as small as your controlling desires or as great as your dominant aspiration.... Dream lofty dreams, and as you dream, so shall you become. Your vision is the promise of what you shall one day be; your ideal is the prophecy of what you shall at last unveil."[3]

WARMTH—incubation/encouragement. If you plant a seed in good soil with plenty of nutrients and minerals and provide lots of water, but the temperature is freezing, there will be no growth. It must have warmth, and warmth encourages growth. Warmth is the soft factor. It encourages and supports. It welcomes new ideas, encourages innovation, and forgives mistakes.

7 CO_2**—exertion/effort.** CO_2 comes from a variety of sources, not the least of which is animal respiration. It's what we exhale and is the result of effort or exertion. Without effort, nothing else matters. In 1999, William Laurance, writing for *Natural History*, made a direct correlation between increased carbon levels in the air and increased growth rates of rainforest trees. Just as extra carbon can grow bigger trees faster, so hard work can bolster the growth rate of any business.[4]

These seven elements work quietly together to produce a life-giving, life-sustaining enterprise. A great idea combined with good information, sufficient capital, clear vision, and hard work, if properly nurtured, will produce a good stream of cash flow and grow any business.

Not only are there seven elements required to turn a seed into a tree and an idea into an established, thriving business, but also each plant goes through seven distinct stages of growth.

1 **Germination:** The idea is acted on. Investment is made. Resources are committed.

2 **Roots down:** The new plant looks for security, sending roots down to get more water (information) and nutrients (capital), gaining stabilization before going to market.

3 **Stems up:** The stems support the leaves. Think of the stems as the leadership team going ahead and opening up the new location or venture that will ultimately support a team of productive workers (leaves). Leaders must lead. They need to go first.

4 **Seek the light:** Keep your eye on the vision. Be vigilant about continuously aligning your strategy with the vision. Position yourself to best pass on the vision to the rest of the team.

5 **Grow leaves:** Build your support staff and get productive. Leaves turn light energy (vision) into chemical energy (action) to produce food (product or service).

6 **Flowers bloom:** Flowers use shape, color, design, and scent to attract pollinators such as birds and bees. Think of the flowers as marketing and the pollinators as early adapters. The pollinators are first to respond to the marketing message, and they carry that message wherever they go. They spread the word on behalf of the marketer. That ultimately brings the next phase.

7 **Grow fruit:** Think of it as critical mass. According to Wikipedia, "Critical mass is a sociodynamic term to describe the existence of sufficient momentum in a social system such that the momentum becomes self-sustaining and fuels further growth."[5] In the rainforest, once fruit is produced, every manner of customer flocks, climbs, and crawls to enjoy its bounty. In the process, the seeds within the fruit are freely distributed on the forest floor, ensuring a self-sustaining condition with continuous future growth.

Once you see it, the rainforest takes on new meaning, new awe, and new excitement as you realize there is an endless supply of exotic plants producing products, attracting customers, competing for limited resources, and utilizing a multitude of strategies to accomplish individual and unified goals—individual because each species must survive on its own merit; unified in the sense that there is interconnectedness in the rainforest of mutual contribution for the common good.

ACTION STEPS

1 Look at anything in nature today and observe what role it plays in the ecosystem it is part of. Consider its importance. Then look to business and ask what or who plays that same role. Begin training yourself to interpret symbols and tap into the wisdom of the ages.

2 List three ideas (seeds) you want to see turned into tangible reality

3 What information (water) do you need to acquire for those dreams to become reality?

4 With whom can you share those ideas who will encourage you?

■   ■   ■   ■

SPONTANEOUS WEALTH
Seeing What Others Miss

Limitations live only in our minds. But if we use our imaginations, our possibilities become limitless.[1]

JAMIE PAOLINETTI

Today the greatest single source of wealth is between your ears.[2]

BRIAN TRACY

He does not possess wealth that allows it to possess him.[3]

BENJAMIN FRANKLIN

BEFORE WEALTH MANIFESTS ITSELF IN TANGIBLE FORM, IT exists first and foremost in an intangible form. What we see with our natural eyes is a manifestation of something that first existed in an unseen state. This book, for example, existed in my mind for a long time before it ever presented itself to you. Another way of saying this is that everything is "twice created"—first in your mind, then in physical form. If you go through life only seeing the effect or the outcome, but never discern the cause of things, you will live at the mercy or lack thereof of those who see into both worlds and move freely between them.

Wealth is first of all an internal possession. If you don't have it on the inside, you will never have it on the outside. You can only manifest in life what you possess on the inside—nothing more. The life you lead on the outside is a reflection of the things you believe and the truths you understand on the inside. The wealth inside this book will become yours in a series of brilliant "Aha!" moments, flashes of revelation borrowed from the oldest, most abundant, diverse, and thriving enterprise on earth— the rainforest. Business fads come and go, but the rainforest has been thriving for eons despite having limited capital (poor topsoil) to work with and now provides us with an unlimited source of renewable wealth to make our world a better, more prosperous place for everyone.

Some years ago in the dead of winter, I took on a new client in a small Midwest town. He picked me up in the morning to take me to his office, which turned out to be a rundown, clapboard house in the poor side of town. When we walked through the front door, the carpet was thick with dog hair and shredded newspaper. I thought it must be where he kept his dog when it got cold and where he stored his construction equipment. As we worked our way through piles of old newspapers and stacks of magazines, we found ourselves in the room he called his office.

He sat down at his desk as I stood awkwardly looking for a chair I could clear off and be seated in. Not finding one and looking intently at him and the disaster that was his office, I asked him a question. "Can I be frank with you?" He winced as he seemed to know what was coming and replied, "I am paying you thousands of dollars. I expect you to be frank with me." With kindness and directness I replied, "This place is a pigsty. There is no point in me helping you bring order to this mess. It's a reflection of the mess on the inside of you. Unless we deal with the mess on the inside of you first, this mess will just come right back!" He agreed, and we left immediately for a restaurant to have breakfast.

We spent the rest of the day at his discretion, identifying the utter poverty and chaos that was on the inside of him. His story was painful and horrific, but completely redeemable. Over the course of our time together, we rooted out the lies that he believed and planted truth in the core of his soul. It was clear by the time I left that he was ready to bring order to his outside world because it had finally come to his inside world. Despite a significant financial inheritance, this man lived in poverty on the outside because that is what he had on the inside. We can only sustainably project to the outside what we consistently have on the inside.

WEALTH WORTH HAVING

Spontaneous wealth is not about magically producing instant, spendable wealth. Rather, it's about producing great wealth on the inside so that you can ultimately produce that wealth on the outside. When I say wealth, it may not be tangible riches. It might be health or relationships, but it could easily include the tangible things of life that are important to you. However, if the driving force of your life is to accumulate things, you will be sorely disappointed even if you are successful at doing this. Life is more than food and drink, houses and cars, boats and planes. David Myers, professor of psychology at Hope College, writes, "More than ever, we have big houses and broken homes, high incomes and low morale, secured rights and diminished civility. We excel at making a living but often fail at making a life. We celebrate our prosperity but yearn for purpose. We cherish our freedoms but long for connection. In an age of plenty, we feel spiritual hunger."[4] If your outer prosperity outstrips your inner wealth, you will find yourself most disillusioned indeed. Spontaneous wealth first of all addresses the inner you so you can well handle what comes at you or to you on the outside.

Drug-dependent celebrities, suicidal CEOs, temperamental tycoons, and others of the rich and famous class aren't the only ones who can testify to this. Harvard University psychologist Daniel Gilbert, in his best-selling *Stumbling on Happiness*, writes, "Psychologists have spent decades studying the relation between wealth and happiness, and they have generally concluded that wealth increases human happiness when it lifts people out of abject poverty and into the middle class but that it does little to increase happiness thereafter." According to Gilbert, "Americans who earn $50,000 per year are much happier than those who earn $10,000 per year, but Americans who earn $5 million per year are not much happier than those who earn $100,000 per year."[5] With more tangible wealth comes much more tangible responsibility, and that can be stressful. As Thomas Jefferson once commented, "It is neither wealth nor splendor, but tranquility and occupation, which give happiness."[6]

The wealth I am speaking of can never be stolen by someone else. It keeps growing with compound interest, can be freely shared without depleting the principal amount, and you can never have too much of it.

The more you have, the more you want to give away. The more you give away, the more you have! This wealth I am speaking of is knowledge, combined with wisdom and understanding. Sometimes the acquisition of that inner wealth occurs in a "suddenly" moment when you least expect it. Coming like a flash, the idea for a new product, service, or idea animates your every gesture as you excitedly sketch out the core concepts you "see" on the inside. I call it spontaneous because it so often occurs in a flash of genius. It's a spark you weren't expecting, much like the spark you sometimes get in wintertime when you rub your feet along the carpet and then touch someone, shocking both of you!

Think of knowledge as static. In many respects, knowledge is the raw material you build with. It's like wood and stone to build a house. It is solid, time tested, proven, and reliable. But it's not enough. You need wisdom. Wisdom factors in everyone's interests and preferences for the house. It considers school location, size of kitchen, safety of neighborhood, resale value, and a host of other factors. Wisdom takes knowledge and makes a sound, logical decision. But that is still not enough. Without understanding, you only have a well-designed house in a good neighborhood. Understanding is that intangible element that makes a house a home! It factors in the emotional impact of things and understands the advantages not just from a logical viewpoint, but also by how it affects everyone's well-being. Wisdom is about *doing* well. Understanding is about well-being. When knowledge, wisdom, and understanding converge in a moment, you have spontaneous wealth, and you are forever impacted by that deposit!

This spontaneous wealth is limitless in scope and supply, and it can occur in an instant. My friend David Johnson of Epiphany Marketing told me the story of his friend who invented a device called the "Signalmatic," which solves a problem for motorcyclists. It turns out that motorcycles have trouble with "smart" traffic lights, because the sensors in the roads (which are basically upside-down metal detectors) frequently do not detect the presence of the motorcycles. The bikes don't have nearly as much metal as cars and trucks do, so the detectors don't pick them up.

This is a source of major frustration for motorcyclists and has resulted in a number of traffic tickets for the bikers who eventually proceed through a red light when there is no traffic and the light won't turn green. Cliff was an inventor and traffic engineer who rode motorcycles. He was frustrated by the problem, but he was convinced there was a way to solve it. After tinkering for a number of years without coming up with a solution, Cliff found himself more and more agitated. Then one night while driving through the mountains of Tennessee in a rainstorm, Cliff had a bizarre experience. It was as if a scroll opened up across his windshield, blocking his view of the road. On the scroll was a schematic (an electrical diagram) for a circuit. It was open in front of Cliff's face long enough for him to comprehend the diagram, and then it disappeared. His first thought was, "That will never work," because the circuit appeared to do nothing but cancel itself out (in a rather complex manner). He went home and built the device, despite his awareness that it should have no effect. Once he had the circuit completed, he attached it to a wooden broomstick and went out to a troublesome traffic signal late at night, and, to his surprise, it "tripped" the traffic light!

Later, when working on patenting the device, Cliff turned everything over to a NASA scientist to help with the technical aspects of the patent application. The NASA scientist told Cliff that not only was his original assessment correct—the device *should do nothing* but cancel itself out from an electrical standpoint—but that they could only conclude that it operated on an as-yet-undiscovered principle of physics. This was the only plausible explanation for the device achieving the desired result.

While it's true that inner wealth can occur spontaneously, it's also a process of diligent study, applied learning, and experimentation. Those "suddenly" moments like the one Cliff experienced are built upon a history of accumulated learning already in place that gives that moment sufficient context to make sense of the sudden revelation. Be that as it may, I believe there is a body of knowledge, a source of wisdom and understanding outside of ourselves, that is accessible to the true seeker. This limitless source of truth is often accessed not by reading books, but by reflective thought, pondering, or meditating on even the simplest of things.

Take, for example, Sir Isaac Newton, one of the foremost scientific intellects of all time. One day he observed an apple fall from a tree. That was nothing new. People had witnessed that and similar events since there were people on the planet. What Sir Isaac did, though, was to meditate, ponder, and consider exactly what he was seeing. He noticed also, that same evening, the moon hanging in the night sky held in place by an invisible force. He concluded that the same thing that caused the apple to fall to the ground was exactly the same thing that held the moon in its orbit.

What he discovered was what we now call the law of gravity. No one taught him this. He accessed that knowledge independent of a textbook, and as a religious man believed things like, "The most beautiful system of the sun, planets, and comets, could only proceed from the counsel and dominion of an intelligent and powerful Being."[7] With that belief in mind, he spent his life accessing that great wealth of knowledge. Near the end of his life he reflected, "I do not know what I may appear to the world; but to myself I seem to have been only like a boy playing on the seashore, and diverting myself in now and then finding of a smoother pebble or a prettier shell than ordinary, whilst the great ocean of truth lay all undiscovered before me."[8] The world is a better place and took great leaps of advancement because of one man with a towering perspective, the curiosity of a child, and a humble heart. The smooth pebbles he discovered on the seashore of life advanced us all.

You don't have to be a genius to encounter genius. When I was five years of age, I was sent to my room for a nap one afternoon. I hated naps because I was never tired in the middle of the afternoon. It wasn't until much later that I discovered it was my mother who was tired of me! Nonetheless, as I lay on my bed imagining things, I began to ponder the concept of movement. In my mind, I saw a red ball traveling in an arc between two points. I knew you could take a picture of a ball in flight and possibly freeze it in flight in a single frame.

I wondered, Does the ball really stop for just an instant? If so, what got it going again? How long was it stationary for? As I began trying to solve this riddle, I saw another picture. It was the same red ball traveling in the same arc but with an infinite number of stops along the way. Though I had yet to hear and learn the meaning of the word *infinite*, I had already observed it in my mind. I just didn't have the vocabulary to explain what I then understood. I hadn't even started school yet! As I later discovered as a teenager reading a book on math and physics, what I saw is exactly what occurs. Motion is an infinite, continuous series of stops even when it has both a starting and ending point.

Now fast-forward to the rainforest with me. Think of it as a physical reality portraying an intangible truth. When you begin to see with the eyes of your understanding instead of relying strictly on your natural eyesight, you gain great vision. You can see in the natural realm *and* in the realm that makes it all work. You go from seeing the things that are made and appreciating them, to seeing the laws or "ways" that *govern* the things that are made. That catapults you from being a mere consumer or user of things created, to having the knowledge, insight, and wisdom to become a co-creator or inventor of a multitude of things. It's like having night-vision goggles in a land with no sun. When you learn how to see on the inside things that are not seen with the natural eye, you gain an incredible advantage in life. That in itself is wealth!

If you want to gain that inner wealth that equips you to manifest the outer wealth you desire, do what Sir Isaac Newton did and recalibrate yourself and your perception of the world around you with the joy and fascination of a child. Step back and get a bigger perspective. Learn how to see the forest *and the* trees. Recognize that you are not the source of all truth, but all truth is accessible by anyone who truly seeks. Become a joyful seeker.

Once you have the wealth of an idea or concept on the inside, then begins the hard work—turning that spontaneous burst of revelation into a tangible reality that really delivers what it promises. While inner wealth can occur quite spontaneously, it may well take a lifetime to incarnate those concepts into reality. But unless the word, idea, or concept becomes flesh, how will it benefit the world? Let's face it; good ideas are a dime a dozen. Great ideas are a nickel apiece! It's the ability to fungigate (transform) those ideas into practical innovations that create value. It's simply not enough to have internal wealth. The great value comes from being able to transform concept to creation.

I get paid handsomely for my advice, input, or ideas, but I can make a fortune if I take that one step further and actually take charge of the process and turn the inspiration into innovation for the client. Thinkers are in low supply and high demand. By that I mean, most people take life as it comes and fall into line with whatever flow they get caught in. Thinkers ask a lot of questions, are often underappreciated, and can easily slow the process down. However, they often come up with great suggestions that will actually improve the process and speed things up if someone will recognize the insight and act upon it.

Doers, on the other hand, should be in high supply but, in fact, are not. The world is full of people who can tell the story, but there are far fewer who can get it done. Consider the sales profession. There seems to be lots of them—no apparent shortage of doers. But when you define a doer as someone who actually executes all the duties from prospecting, proposal writing, follow-up, thank-you notes, closing the sale, delivering the value proposition, and good record keeping, they are few and far between. Most are more talk than walk. If you want to know where the real opportunity is, become a thinker *and* a doer. Walk by revelation *and* by sight. Be a person of inspiration *and* innovation! If you are a consultant, you can charge one fee for advice but an entirely different fee for a result. Most people don't want advice. They want someone to "fix it" *for them*, to make their problem go away or make their dream come true. Don't just be the one who can point the way...lead the way. Make it happen, and get paid accordingly!

Spontaneous wealth is that magical "Aha!" moment when you suddenly realize you have the solution to a difficult problem. It may be a great idea for a new revenue stream or a new way of presenting an old idea. It might be a simple way to accomplish what has been heretofore a difficult and challenging process. Years ago, early in my consulting career, I was asked by a national manufacturer if I would train the supervisors, foremen, and managers at a factory that made hydraulic cylinders. They were experiencing just over one hundred late orders every day. That meant that on any given day, there were one hundred customer orders in production that were running later than promised. Naturally, this was disconcerting to both the customers and the manufacturer.

The owner had tried everything for over a decade to improve their late-order status, including courses, video training, process experts, and so on. It was really more out of desperation that I was invited to help. The owner was hoping that perhaps my sales training principles, for which I was known, could somehow apply to manufacturing. I accepted the challenge, but the night before the Saturday training, I realized I had made the cardinal mistake of letting the client diagnose the problem *and* prescribe the solution. While he was certainly qualified to make the correct diagnosis, his track record proved his prescriptions were not on target. And now, late at night in my hotel, I realized what I was about to present was all wrong. I desperately needed an "Aha!" moment. I needed a deposit of spontaneous wealth about a topic that none of my training or professional experience had ever prepared me for.

On literally the wings of a hope and a prayer, I stood the next morning in front of a group of seasoned veterans who knew more about their job and process than I would ever learn in the rest of my years. But I had an "Aha!" It was an idea. A thought. A real inspiration. Spontaneous wealth. I simply asked a few questions, beginning with, "What number of late orders is acceptable?" If cutting that rate in half was acceptable, they would never get there. I helped them see that ZERO late orders was the *only* acceptable number. Then we looked at causes. Predictably, production was slow because the other guy was always late delivering the part being worked on in the manufacturing process. Everyone had an excuse and no one was on the hook.

I challenged them to change that. I suggested they each assume 100 percent responsibility for every order. If something was late coming to them, go after it. Don't accept excuses from others or from themselves. I had no clue how to change the manufacturing process or whether there was a better way to organize manufacturing equipment so things flowed through the process more smoothly. What I did know was that everyone had an excuse, and until "zero late orders" was the only acceptable standard, there would always be an abundance of late orders coupled with an abundance of seemingly bona fide excuses.

The next week, late orders fell into the twenties for the first time in over a decade. The second week, it was cut by a further 50 percent! It wasn't because of some great wisdom I had studied to acquire, but rather from a spontaneous "Aha!" moment where wealth was deposited in me. From there, I knew how to transfer that wealth to others who had the practical knowledge to incarnate that revelation into actionable steps resulting in profound change!

The magnificence of the rainforest is that it is dripping with golden "Aha!" moments just waiting to be picked. Every tree has a story to tell. Every plant has a message to give. Every flower dances gloriously in the afternoon breeze, proclaiming a wisdom and wealth it freely gives to all who seek. But you have to humble yourself from your Ivy League education and learn to see the created order through a new lens. You must be willing to be tutored by a system that predates recorded history and functions by a set of principles, strategies, and rules we are not wise enough to invent. You must close your eyes and see, plug your ears and hear, shut your mouth and let the wisdom speak. And you must listen.

Inner wealth, to have any recognizable value, must be spent. It is in spending your inner wealth that it even becomes visible and believable to others. When you get a fresh deposit of newfound wealth on the inside, as quickly as possible find a way to put that into action and transactionalize it. Fungigate (transform) it. That is when it becomes beneficial to yourself and others. Knowledge without action is lifeless. Wisdom without use is folly. Bread that is not eaten turns moldy. Prove, test, and try the inner wealth you have much as a swordsman tests and tries his new armor and sword before going into battle.

Not all "revelations" you get are brilliant. Some are downright dim and ill conceived, but in the testing of them, the fuller picture comes into play. We often see through a glass darkly. Sometimes however, it's the ill-conceived brain flash that leads to the well-conceived innovation. The point here is to test all your ideas before trying to export them. As you attempt to convert your inner wealth to outer wealth, you automatically increase your inner wealth by virtue of use, much as muscles develop with use. That in turn increases your potential for outer wealth. And so the cycle continues.

I stated at the onset that no one can steal your inner wealth. Because of that, even your outer wealth has a certain amount of security. If you lose it, you will likely have accrued more inner wealth by then and through that experience can more readily reacquire what you formerly had in tangible form. About twenty-five years ago, I lost just about everything a person can lose except his health. I had started a business with some partners, and we went upside down very quickly. In just a few months I owed hundreds of thousands of dollars, and my partners quickly filed for bankruptcy protection. As they did, their share of the debt fell to me, and the load got unbearably heavy. Although I lacked the wealth of knowledge to avoid that predicament, I was fortunate enough to have gained some inner wealth along the way that got me through.

WEALTH THROUGH PAIN

It came from my daughter Jennifer Lynn, who was born with Down syndrome and a hole in her heart. For some reason, the only thing I had ever truly feared at a deep level was that someday I would have a child with this condition. It was not a reasonable fear, but it was very real, and truly, what I feared greatly came upon me. The first morning after getting her home from the hospital, I laid her on the living room floor, wrapped in her pink blanket. She was totally unaware of her problems and was peacefully cooing away, unaware of my shock and grief.

As I gazed at her, with tears falling from my face, it occurred to me that unconditional love was meant to be unconditional. If God could love us that way, I should extend that same kind of love to her. It felt like a backhoe had dug a merciless hole in my chest cavity, and the hole was filling with water. I thought I would suffocate until that still small voice reminded me that every adversity carries with it an equal or greater opportunity, that my daughter was a blessing and not a curse. I saw that her handicap was only a problem to me, and I needed to change my thinking.

It was then I realized that everyone else I knew got stuck with "normal" kids, but I had this incredible opportunity to grow and mature and gain wisdom far beyond my years. I knew in an instant that getting through the challenges that would and did inevitably present themselves would make me into the man I always wanted to be. I was blessed to enjoy her smile for eighteen months before she died a week before Christmas in 1979 after a failed attempt to repair the hole in her heart. Her departure from this earth fixed the hole in her heart while leaving one in mine. That hole soon filled with water, forming a well of compassion and understanding from which I have drunk deeply on occasion and, at times, nourished others.

Here it was just two and a half years later, and my first real push into a real business with a real line of credit, a warehouse, office, and lots of staff was now defunct. Remembering the inner wealth I had obtained courtesy of my daughter Jennifer, I recognized this new trial as another adversity joined at the hip to another opportunity. Though I would never have signed up for that trial, I looked at my financial indebtedness as an investment in my education. I knew for me to file for bankruptcy would mean I would miss too many lessons, that I wouldn't learn a fraction of what I would learn by going through the fire. I believed if I walked through the fire of affliction that I was less likely to make the same mistakes again, but if I took the shortcut, I would not learn the lessons and would be doomed to repeat my mistakes. In short, I was building inner wealth so I would have another shot at succeeding on the outside.

Inner wealth is something that presents itself to you in disguise. You see a tree. Learn to see its meaning, what it could represent, such as a business model. You see the sunlight. Learn to see the power of vision. You see the rain. Learn to see abundance of information and knowledge. You see the pain. Learn to see the gain. In one sense, we live in a dualistic world with alternate realities. The physical world is discerned by the five senses, and the nonphysical is discerned by our inner being. When you see adversity, don't leave it until you find the opportunity. It is always there. No coin has just one side. You wouldn't know light without darkness. You wouldn't know wet without dry. And you won't know opportunity without adversity. In fact, opportunity is always guarded by adversity or problems. The greater the opportunity, the more challenging and difficult the adversity you must overcome. It is in the overcoming of the adversity that you acquire the skills to steward the opportunity wisely.

There is a huge payoff in adjusting your perspective to seeing both the material and nonmaterial world and knowing how to operate within both simultaneously. When my wife and I had a small book publishing company, we had published our first book, called *The Bible Incorporated* (www.BibleIncorporated.com). It was a big deal for us. We had no financing, so we had to presell books to have enough money to pay for the print run. This particular book, which went on to become a big best seller for us, was originally only available in leather and sold for twenty dollars.

On our third print run, we had secured all the necessary presell orders to be able to pay for the book when it came off the press in a print run of twenty-five thousand copies. On the day the press was to begin running, our largest pre-order of five thousand books was canceled. I was devastated because now I had no way of paying for the books when they came off the press. I called my wife and told her the great news. I explained that this was a very painful adversity with potentially business-ending ramifications and therefore had incredible potential and opportunity because adversity and opportunity are *always* joined at the hip! She came to the office so we could quiet our minds and hearts to find the wisdom and see the opportunity. Before the day was over, we changed our book order to five thousand leather books, and for the first time ever, we introduced a paperback edition with twenty thousand printed in that format and for a much lower cost, of course. It went on to become our best-selling version and had our best margins. It truly was an opportunity disguised as a problem. In solving it, we reaped a bountiful harvest!

Spontaneous wealth is synonymous to inner growth. If you want to experience wealth on the outside that doesn't deplete you on the inside, you need to accumulate some inner wealth. Here are some basic steps to build up your wealth on the inside:

1. **Take responsibility for your condition.** Clean house on the inside. Rid yourself of "stinking thinking." Eliminate the poverty on the inside. Make no place for it. Tear down old ways of negative thinking. You know what they are. Replace the negative thoughts and beliefs with truth. Think on those things.

2. **Invest in yourself.** Become an avid learner. Charlie "Tremendous" Jones claims, "You are the same today you'll be in five years except for two things: the people you meet and the books you read."[9]

Rediscover your childlikeness. Be curious again. Walk in the woods. Come with me to the rainforest. Explore the Sonoran Desert. Watch National Geographic. Turn all the lights off in the house, step outside in the night sky, lie down on a blanket, and count the stars. Take up painting or sculpting. Write a short story. Observe a bird in flight. Buy an orchid. Ask a million questions. Expect an answer.

 Act on what you receive. If it doesn't work out, what is the worst that can happen? Like Thomas Edison once said, "If I find 10,000 ways something won't work, I haven't failed. I am not discouraged, because every wrong attempt discarded is another step forward."[10]

ACTION STEPS

1 Ask the following question: What lie do you believe about yourself that is limiting you or holding you back? Don't rush this. Wait patiently. Write down the answer.

2 Then ask this: What is the truth about yourself that should replace that lie? People talk about a higher power all the time. I believe in that unseen Higher Power, and I am convinced He reveals Himself to those who seek Him in sincerity. Try it.

3 For the next week, set aside one hour of the day that is normally unproductive, like television time or Internet time, and give yourself some good input from books or by picking the brain of someone you admire, or by simply going for a walk and recalibrating your inner self.

4 Identify one adversity facing you right now and look for the opportunity that is most certainly attached to it. State the problem, and then write a list of possible opportunities that exist. Come up with at least five good positive, meaningful outcomes that could occur from this adversity.

WEALTH SECRET #1:

THE FUNGUS FACTOR
Getting the Most From the Least

> …the most complex ecosystem on earth…the tropical rainforest is one thousand times more biologically complex than the tropical reef system, the second most complex system on earth, with one million times greater biodiversity than our own ecosystem here.[1]
>
> MIKE ROBINSON, Director of National Zoo

WHEN YOU STEP INSIDE THE RAINFOREST, YOU TAKE A STEP back in time—so far back, it seems that time itself is no longer a factor. There are no clocks hanging on trees. No sundials in the clearings. No sense of time or urgency. Yet everything is progressing, producing, busily moving along at the speed of peace. Peace. That is the overwhelming and immediate experience you encounter once you step inside the rainforest. It quiets every distraction in your mind, and you are absorbed into a sea of green and peace. The tranquility is compelling *and* instructive.

I remember visiting Cathedral Forest, the old-growth rainforest on Vancouver Island in British Columbia, with Douglas firs towering three hundred feet, big enough it seemed you could build a subdivision with each one! The fascinating thing was that everyone walking through that forest was whispering in soft, respectful tones. Nobody told them to do that. It just seemed like the thing to do. Nobody wanted to disturb the profound peace we were corporately experiencing in that remarkable rainforest.

Here's the instructive part: rainforests thrive in an environment of peace, and so will we. When we are in peace, it is far easier to discern the still, small voice that belongs to the One who created the rainforest. Trees aren't stressed out about whether there will be enough rain or whether their fruit will ever mature. They simply do what they were designed to do, and the result is predictable and abundant. It's a bit like the Amazon River looking for all the world peaceful on the surface, gently winding its way through the rainforest, while all the while quietly and efficiently moving 4.2 million cubic feet of silt and 32 million gallons of water *per second* out into the Atlantic Ocean.

When we are in a place of peace, it strengthens our ability to concentrate so we make better decisions and can focus on the activity that produces results instead of fretting over something we can't change anyway. Furthermore, researchers at the American Institute of Stress estimate that 60 to 80 percent of accidents on the job are stress related. When you factor in accidents; absenteeism; employee turnover; diminished productivity; direct medical, legal, and insurance costs; workers' compensation; and legal settlements, workplace stress is costing U.S. industry an estimated $300 billion annually.[2] Peace is an inner condition you can choose in the midst of turmoil, chaos, and confusion. In fact, that's when you need it most. If you find yourself lacking that peace, consider taking a walk in the woods, quiet your soul, and reacquaint yourself with the presence of peace.

THE MYTH OF PERPETUAL GROWTH

One reason we don't have peace is because we try to be something we're not. We want to be like Microsoft or Starbucks when perhaps we're best suited to be like that one-of-a-kind fish market in Seattle (Pike's Place Fish Market) where they throw fish to each other and the customers. They are not on every corner like Starbucks, but people from every corner of the world come there to partake of their bounty and enjoy the experience.

One of the first things that strike you in the rainforest is the diversity. Tropical rainforests cover an estimated 2–7 percent of the earth's surface (depending on whose estimation) and yet contain over two-thirds of the earth's plant species![3] Everywhere you look, it's something different, something beautiful, something totally unique—and it's thriving in the midst of hundreds of competitors.

Trees in the rainforest have no preconception about dominating the market or taking over the forest. They thrive by fulfilling their destiny, their role, their niche. Like any other successful business, they start out with a seed, put their roots down with limited working capital, and get to work producing what they were simply meant to produce. They succeed, in part, because they produce a quality product on a consistent basis, year in and year out, and their customers keep coming back for their fruit or their nectar or simply for the comfort of their shade.

The goal is not perpetual growth, but a continuous commitment to become fully what you were designed best to become. Here's the good news: you don't have to be the biggest to be a success. You don't have to dominate the market to be a winner. Find what you do best. Do it consistently. Thrive where you are planted. Serve where you're celebrated. Be at peace with what you are best suited for, and do it with all your heart!

Rainforests are not worried about time, yet they operate on a timetable. It seems paradoxical. They absorb light in the day, not because of a clock, but because that's when the sun is out. The forest has a rhythm and doesn't need a clock. Time is a means of measuring the rhythm, not controlling it. I like what Golda Meir, former prime minister of Israel, said, "I must govern the clock, not be governed by it."[4] One of the keys to high productivity is finding the rhythm and dancing with it.

Rainforests are never late or early. They know all about JIT (just in time). Small suppliers (small trees, shrubs, etc.) provide materials (organic waste) for big manufacturers (larger trees) who employ specialists (fungus) to convert that waste into usable supply (food, products) and keep things moving. The interconnectivity and interdependence in the rainforest defies comprehension. Everything is linked to everything else, it seems. All individual accomplishment is done in a context of group participation or teamwork, and productivity soars. You never see a rainforest stressing about output. All energies are focused on keeping the main thing, the main thing, while consistently working with excellence.

Collective input, reliable supply, and focus on the right things seem to produce the best results.

Xenophon A. Koufteros from the University of Texas at El Paso and Mark A. Vonderembse and William J. Doll of the University of Toledo did an interesting research paper titled, "How to Cut Manufacturing Throughput Time." They did a study of 244 discrete part manufacturing firms primarily from four industries: fabricated metal products, industrial and commercial machinery, electrical equipment, and transportation equipment. They concluded three major lessons from that study:[5]

1 Throughput time increases in an organizational climate that encourages employee empowerment and participation.

2 Building a base of dependable suppliers is critical for manufacturing competitiveness.

3 Keep your eye on the "right" ball. Managers need to focus their actions on reengineering setups, cellular manufacturing, preventive maintenance, and quality-improvement efforts rather than on outcomes such as reducing inventory and cutting costs.

The purpose of the study was to learn how to increase throughput in a manufacturing environment. The quicker you turn over resources, the more times you can repeat the process and the more profit you can generate from that process. If you have processes that are moving inefficiently, you can benefit greatly from the tropical rainforest model. A key to success is the rapid turnover of nutrients. Let me explain.

The rainforest thrives in large part because of a relatively obscure process where fungus (90 percent of which live beneath the surface and are attached to the roots) converts waste and dead organic matter to nutrients the plant or tree can utilize and profit from. In cooler climates, a leaf falls to the ground and may still be there a year later, but in the tropical rainforest it is recycled back into useful supply in as little as thirty days. For that to occur, the leaf must be broken down into its basic organic and mineral components. That is the role of the fungus—turning under-utilized or discarded or nonfunctioning assets into a life-sustaining flow of nutrients and minerals—cash. It is far more than simply selling off dead inventory or disposing of underutilized real estate.

Before we go further down this important road, you need to under-stand why the tropical rainforest is the most diverse, abundant, and fruitful ecosystem on the planet. How it differs from a temperate rain-forest like the ones I have visited in British Columbia with their towering, nine-hundred-year-old Douglas firs, which were hundreds of feet tall when Columbus discovered America, is key to understanding the vital components for building a thriving business.

There are several conditions required for a tropical rainforest to produce abundance. Primarily, there needs to be light, warmth, and moisture.

1. Abundant sunlight: speaks to *inspiration* (vision)

Tropical rainforests wrap around the globe along the equator like a belt with little variation in the amount of sunlight during the day throughout the year. The time for sunrise and sunset doesn't vary more than about an hour of the same time every day. Because of their location, they don't have months with limited daylight hours followed by seasons of longer days. The light they receive is consistent, every day of the year. Light speaks of vision, and keeping a consistent vision is key to success. Of course, vision grows and modifies over time, but changing the vision every year or every season or every week, depending on the opportunities you have in front of you, creates instability and stunts growth.

Vision provides the energy needed to break the inertia and begin to take action. Set aside time to get clear on your vision. See it. Think it. Write it. Speak it. Make it part of the regular corporate discussion. Understand that your vision will change as you gain perspective (height). What you see for your future today will grow and evolve over time, slowly becoming something you didn't fully see when you began. Make sure to review your vision often and let it grow with you.

2. Warm temperatures: speaks to *incubation* (encouragement)

Constant sunlight results in higher temperatures that vary little during the year. The temperature on the constantly shaded rainforest floor will vary even less. Not only are tropical rainforests warm; they are consistently warm. That warm, nurturing environment is similar to the controlled environment of an incubator used to nurture premature babies. The incubator creates an artificial or temporary environment of nurturing and support until the baby can live outside that environment. In business, this speaks to a welcoming, stable environment where encouragement is practiced, innovation is welcome, and new ideas are explored. A word of encouragement during a failure is worth more than an hour of praise after success.

Create a culture of encouragement that is willing to give new ideas a chance, a culture that encourages life and creativity and is a safe place to introduce new concepts. Toyota solicited in-house wisdom for improving their manufacturing (instead of outside resources), and by 1982 they were getting two suggestions per month per employee and implementing 95 percent of them.[6] (They make Lexus!) William Arthur Ward, one of America's most quoted writers of inspirational maxims, wrote, "Flatter me, and I may not believe you. Criticize me, and I may not like you. Ignore me, and I may not forgive you. Encourage me, and I will not forget you."[7]

Lou Holtz, former NCAA football and NFL head coach, distinguished himself by being the only coach in NCAA history to lead six different programs to bowl games and guide four different programs to final top twenty rankings. The story of how he got from being the smallest and least suited player on his high school football team to the fame he now enjoys hinges upon a single conversation of encouragement provided by his high school coach. Apparently his coach was leaving for a bigger opportunity and called Holtz and his parents into a meeting to suggest that Holtz go to college and pursue a career as a football coach instead of a player. No one in the family had even thought he would go to college, let alone become a football coach, but that one encouraging conversation changed the direction of his life. The family pitched in together and sent him to Kent State University.[8] The rest, as they say, is history. Never underestimate the power of encouragement!

Years ago I was visiting some friends in British Columbia. One morning as I was in the kitchen getting some coffee, their young son Jordan was at the kitchen table looking depressed as he studied for his weekly spelling test of twenty words. He explained to me that he was not one of the smart kids at school and that each week he barely passed his test, getting from ten to fifteen words right out of twenty. I asked him who told him he was not one of the smart kids. Apparently it was just understood because he could never spell all the words correctly. His parents worked with him diligently to help him learn the words, but nothing seemed to work.

I let Jordan, who was about seven or eight years old, know that I was an expert in judging people's abilities and talents. I told him that was one of the things companies paid me to do, and as an expert I assured him that people were wrong about him. He really was a bright kid, full of life and energy, brimming with possibilities, but he believed a lie about himself. I explained that he was, in fact, smarter than most kids. He was so smart that he that simply got ahead of himself when he would read or try to spell. Super smart kids, I told him, have to learn how to slow down because they are so incredibly quick with their minds.

I gave Jordan a couple of pointers for slowing down, and then to prove this would work, I told him that if he got a perfect score that day, I would give him ten dollars. I was working with his father that day, and just before his father took me to the airport to fly home, he got a call from a very excited Jordan who had scored, for the first time, a perfect 100 percent! Not only was he calling to share his good news, but I think he wanted his father to make sure he collected the ten dollars from me as well. But it doesn't end there. Each week for several weeks thereafter, not only did Jordan prove his genius by continuing to achieve 100 percent on his subsequent tests, but also before each test he got financial commitments from his parents and grandparents on both sides, and anyone else who would ante up, for a financial reward if he got a perfect score. I knew that kid was a genius!

Not only did Jordan make some fast bucks, but much more importantly, he also broke off a wrong belief and accepted a new image of himself because of one encouraging conversation. It wasn't that no one loved him or that no one wanted to help. The boy needed his confidence raised. Merriam Webster's online dictionary defines *encourage* as "the raising of one's confidence especially by an external agency." It literally means to fill with courage or strength of purpose.

How many of the people who work with or for you have the smarts but lack the confidence? Everyone struggles with that issue on some level. If you want to see productivity soar, use the power of encouragement. Find a way to raise their confidence. One way to do that is to reduce or eliminate the penalty for making a mistake. Reward creativity and extra effort. Draw out of them the good things you see. Reward the behavior you want to see manifest. The process may look something like this:

1. **Observe:** Pay attention to their work, their body language, their attitude, and so on. You can tell when their heart is not in it.

2. **Inquire:** Take an interest in them. Be genuine. Ask questions. Find out what's bothering them.

3. **Listen:** Repeat back what you think you heard them say. Listen to learn.

4. **Empathize:** Put yourself in their shoes. Identify with them.

5. **Deny and correct:** Any perceptions based on lies should be called out and corrected.

6. **Minimize and offset:** Where perceptions are based on truth but are harmful, put them in perspective. Change the emphasis from what they can't do to what they can do well.

7. **Affirm:** Let them know you believe in them, that you are proud of them and know they can do it. Consider giving a one-time incentive for accomplishment if they prove you right.

One last but very important thought on encouragement: Sometimes you just have to encourage yourself. There are times when no one else cares or understands, or, worse yet, they are against you. When you are in that position, remember David and Goliath. No one really believed David would win. His brothers despised him. His friends doubted him. His enemies defied him. He had to encourage himself by recalling past victories where he had killed both a lion and a bear when they attacked the sheep. He denied and corrected what Goliath was saying the outcome was going to be, and he verbalized aloud for everyone to hear (including himself) how Goliath would meet his demise. After filling himself with courage, he acted accordingly and ran toward Goliath (the thing that was taunting him) and slew him.

3. Abundant rain: speaks to *information* (knowledge)

Rainforests create 50 percent of their own rain. While temperate rain-forests have lots of rain, they lack consistent light and warmth and can never produce the abundance and diversity of a tropical rainforest. Water is analogous to information/communication. Half of the rain a rainforest receives comes from outside sources like the ocean, and the other half comes from its own process of transpiration where water evaporates from the leaves back into the air.

Put in business terms, a highly productive business relies on outside sources for only 50 percent of its information. The other 50 percent comes from feedback from every level of the company. This may occur when marketing listens to feedback from the field sales force. It occurs when customer service provides feedback to the sales team. It occurs when accounts receivable shares valuable information with various depart-ments in a company, and so on. Sadly, most companies have very poor internal communication. They have no system for gathering, evaluating, and disseminating helpful information.

We tend to view the world through our own eyes only; rarely do we take the time to try and see it through the lens of another. Do you know why your customers buy from you? Some of them buy for the same reasons you would buy your product or service, but many have different answers. Have you ever surveyed your customer base to find out why they buy from you? You might be surprised at what you learn. Information is unique in that it has the capacity to create value. Furthermore, when combined with other information it can multiply understanding and wealth. If you give information away, you are not depleted for doing so, and if the recipient of that information combines it with theirs, learns something new, and shares that with you, you have increased your wealth again.

Here's a little known secret that can make you prosperous: Everyone knows by looking at their own backyard that things green up and grow up when it rains. The Amazon rainforest, however, puts on its biggest growth spurt during the dry season when it receives the most direct sunlight with little or no rain. How is this possible when most forests in the world drop their leaves during dry season? Here's how: The undisturbed, old-growth rainforests in the Amazon tend to have deep roots and can reach water even in the dry season, allowing the trees to flourish during the sunnier part of the year. They access a store of water (information) deep underground that other forests cannot reach. As a result, they get the best of two vital resources—water and light—simultaneously. In business, it's the power of vision combined with deep wells of information or know-how.

RETAINING WHAT YOU LEARN

Here's how this will help you. Solomon once said that a wise man will store up knowledge. Most people let knowledge pass right through them. They read a book, watch a movie, hear a name, and then promptly forget what they took in. Forget about telling you what the book was about, or even its name; they don't even remember reading it! You must find a way to store the information (knowledge) deep within where you can access it when others are experiencing a mental drought. If you do this, you will be thought a genius when the truth is that you simply remembered what you learned over the years!

Think of it another way. The dry season is really a period of prolonged sunny weather. Sunshine is analogous to vision, revelation, and great purpose. If you don't have the information or know-how (water reservoir) deep within, you will be burned up by the dream, frustrated because you don't know how to make it a reality, or you will become dormant, entering into a period of inactivity, not knowing how to execute it, and lacking the information to proceed. The trees (companies or individuals) with the most deep stored-up water (information) prosper while those with the least actually wither. Bottom line: the most lush rainforest on the planet teaches us that trees with the deepest stores of water (information) are best prepared to take advantage of full-on sunlight, (vision, new ideas, flashes of genius).

When you first read something new and interesting, it's like taking a cool, refreshing shower on a hot day. For as long as you stand under the shower and for a few minutes after, you feel quite refreshed and energized. Two hours later, most of the refreshed feeling is gone, and it's not much longer before every trace of that shower is long forgotten. When you take in information without a mechanism for retaining it, it all goes down the drain, except for a slight lingering memory like the title or perhaps one striking story.

What you want is to be able to put a plug in the drain and keep the water in the tub and soak in it until your fingers and toes look like prunes. It's valuable information that can change your life, and you are choosing to enjoy it only once and then you let it go down the drain. Let me ask you a question. Have you ever been stung by a wasp? Can you remember the first time you were stung as a child? The answer is probably yes, but you probably can't remember the first book you read or even the last one, if it's been more than a year. So we are going to borrow some memory-enhancing techniques I call the WASP strategy. It's easy to remember and will help you retain important information you need to fulfill the vision you were born to fulfill. Take a look and follow the advice.

1. Write it.

Journal your thoughts. Write down the salient points that meant the most to you. On some occasions I have even prepared a book report or summary with the key points that I took out of the book, complete with possible applications, inspired ideas, and so on. Then I printed it out and put it in a binder for easy access with other similar material. Maybe for you the simple solution is to record the best points in your journal, but the simple act of writing out the main points helps you remember and gives you an easy place to locate the information you found valuable instead of leafing through a three-hundred-page book.

2. Apply it.

As quickly as possible, when you learn something new that you see value in, make a point of using that information in a practical way. If possible, use it repeatedly in different ways until it is ingrained into you. According to ScienceAlert.com, neuroscientists at the University of Queensland have just published findings that add more weight to the "use it or lose it" model for brain function, claiming "that if a cell is not appropriately stimulated by other cells, it self-destructs."[9]

Rutgers University reports:

> From the MacArthur and other longitudinal studies has come a guiding principle known as "use it or lose it." A recent brain-scanning study appeared to show this principle in action. As reported in the January 22, 2004 *Nature*, 23 healthy people, average age 22, learned how to juggle. After three months, MRI scans showed enlargement of the gray matter in their brains—the part responsible for higher mental functions. Either existing cells had grown denser, more numerous connections, or the sheer number of brain cells had increased. When the study participants stopped juggling, their brains shrunk again. This doesn't mean we should all juggle our way to cognitive vitality. But it does strongly suggest that mental exercise has real and positive effects on brain function.[10]

If we could recall what we have already learned and were using it, we would have a tremendous advantage in business and life. The easiest way for me to do that is to seal it into my mind by repeated use. The reason using your knowledge works is because of how memory works. When new information is simply told to us or read by us, we don't know where in memory to store it because we don't really comprehend the use of that data. When we experience the information by doing it, we also experience a host of other data input from sight and sound to sensation and taste, even emotional feelings and association to other things we have experienced. Doing what we learn gives us the context to help us categorize the information so we can store it in our memory in an easy-to-access way. The Greek philosopher Sophocles once said, "One must learn by doing the thing; for though you think you know it, you have no certainty, until you try."[11] Modern learning theorist Carl Ransom Rogers (1902–1987) believed that "significant" learning is experiential. The application of the knowledge "addresses the needs and wants of the learner."[12]

3. Speak it.

Another great way to retain valuable information is to immediately share it with others in every context and conversation that makes sense. Better yet, teach it to someone. Seneca wrote in his letters to Lucilius that we are learning if we teach.[13] Give a talk in front of a group on what you learned. In my early copier sales days, every salesman had to come to the sales meeting prepared to teach the rest of us the merits and benefits of a new product or feature. The preparation for teaching the material combined with the act of delivering it caused us to "get it" and retain it much better than we otherwise would.

For example, I first learned about vision and mission as it relates to business because a client many years ago asked me to lead their executive team in a training exercise. I bought every resource I could, studied hard, and prepared diligently, and when the training was complete, they told me it was the best investment they had made of this nature. Teaching is a great way to learn. Take this book, for example; teach your kids about the science part of this. Teach your spouse, friend, or co-worker about the business application. Share your findings in an online discussion group. Start a blog. Do something. Tell someone. Your future benefit depends on it!

4. Ponder it.

I consider this the least effective unless done in conjunction with one of the previous methods, but at the very least, the longer you keep your mind marinating in what you have read, the more likely you are to retain it. Think through the ramifications of what you read, the possible applications, even the veracity of the content. Think how you would do it better, write it better, or somehow improve the content. The longer your mind is engaged on the topic, the better the chances of recalling it later.

Information, like water, causes rapid growth, and the good news is that you don't have to wait until it rains to acquire more information. You can water your mind anytime you like. Most natural resources decline with use, but information is regenerative: the more you use, the more you have. In both the rainforest and business, information triumphs over scarcity. As limits are approached, living systems must adapt or perish. As Plato said in his best-known dialogue, *The Republic*, "Necessity is the mother of invention."[14] When adaptation takes place, information is of necessity acquired and stored, rendering the participant wiser, wealthier, and better prepared for the future.

Where are you getting your information? Only from outside resources? Only from yourself? Broaden your horizons. Engage in dialogue. Get feedback from your staff, family, customers, former customers, and so on. How aggressive are you about learning? Do you wait until it presents itself to you, or do you proactively choose to be a learner? Wise men lay up knowledge, but fools are destroyed for lack of it. It's your choice.

THE KEY TO EVERYTHING—FUNGIGATION

These three things—consistent light, consistent warmth, and abundance of rain—set the stage for the miracle process I call fungigation. It is simply the rapid turnover of nutrients from unusable form to usable. Here's how it works: Fungus and bacteria thrive in the warm, moist climate and immediately feed upon fallen leaves, fruit, and other organic matter, digesting them and depositing the minerals back on the shallow root system of the host tree, usually within a few weeks. By breaking down dead organic material, they continue the cycle of nutrients through ecosystems and keep the rainforest working very efficiently, despite their shallow, relatively infertile topsoil.

In effect, fungi are specialists (niche enterprises) that support the whole. They specialize in the art of transforming the contribution of others into usable, actionable, *beneficial outcomes*. Notice the emphasis on beneficial outcomes. As I said earlier, ideas are a dime a dozen, and great ones are a nickel apiece. But turning them into realities that contribute to the bottom line is rare—and very valuable! Fungi specialize in innovation. The more vision (light), encouragement (warmth), and knowledge (water) you have, the better able you will be to transform lost profit and under-utilized potential (waste) into real and immediate profit, creating as a by-product increased demand for your talent and services.

In the rainforest, waste is provision for something else. In business, waste is lost profit. It's something you paid for but can't use. In nature, a leaf falls to the ground, and right there, it's converted to something else, which is converted to something else, and eventually some of that material becomes a leaf again. Nothing is lost. Where are you creating waste in your business? If you have a service business, one of your biggest waste areas is time. Where can you gain operational efficiencies? What processes can you put in place to redeem your time? These are things we discuss in future chapters.

Kiuchi and Shireman, in their groundbreaking book *What We Learned in the Rainforest: Business Lessons from Nature*, reported that Coors examined every form of waste in their production process. They turned spent grains into fertilizer. Organic waste was sold as compost. Aluminum cans were recycled. They tracked their use of toxic materials, leading to innovations that led to an 80 percent reduction. They invented an ultraviolet process that cured inks in less than a second on their cans, compared to two minutes of baking in energy-hungry ovens, and were able to cut ink consumption by 90 percent.[15]

As good and valuable as recycling is, fungigating goes much deeper. In nature, fungigating is where fungus converts waste into nutrients to resupply the tree or plant. In business, fungigating is the process of breaking down products, services, ideas, systems, and processes that have completed their useful life, and recombining the useful elements in different form for renewed usefulness! It is about far more than mere recycling of physical products. Fungi are innovators or specialists, and in business there is huge need for specialists or innovators to convert waste (unrealized, untapped potential, lost profit) into cash to resupply the company.

Want to get your hands on some capital? Learn to fungigate. Look for lost profit in any form you can find it, from stagnant inventory to underutilized real estate to untapped potential in your staff, and convert those to cash. It's easier than you think. I had a major client get behind in their payables to me. That caused me a temporary squeeze, so I had to make an adjustment. I already knew that in the rainforest, limits are an essential catalyst to improve, develop, and change. Limits look like problems but are, in fact, wonderful opportunities for growth and development of new products or services.

We needed a temporary fix to boost our cash flow, so I met with one of our staff members who is highly talented and in some ways underutilized. We came up with a plan to offer his technical know-how in groups of ten over a series of early-morning conference calls to help subscribers to my e-mail coaching have access to his knowledge and begin applying it to their business. We sent out the e-mail and, within a few days, set a record for the most folks joining an ongoing program like this. Besides providing my readers with access to great information and additional coaching, it immediately resolved our short-term cash requirement simply by looking for excess talent that was going unused.

When the marketplace was converting from audiocassette to CD, we found ourselves with some dead inventory sitting in stock and no demand. We created a special promotion for those folks who still had cassette players and made them an offer they didn't refuse. In hours, we had turned something that had become dead to us into cash flow.

Perhaps the biggest and most amazing example of that is the work I do with a nonprofit foundation. They are the ones raising an endowment to build a revolutionary new model for an international business school. I oversee the endowment raising and get to interact with a remarkable team of highly talented professionals who are passionate about the vision. Our initial goal was a $100 million in endowment value, and the model we have chosen embodies so many of the rainforest principles you will read about. The basic method of raising the endowment is not through bake sales and car washes. It is through the acquisition of underutilized commercial real estate.

Companies ranging from the Fortune 100 to small LLCs transfer title of their hard-to-move real estate assets that no longer serve a need for them to the foundation. In return, the foundation facilitates a 561

Exchange, providing a cash benefit that often exceeds the cash benefit they would get selling it at list price! The corporation gets tremendous value and they get it immediately. They end their carry costs of the empty building. They end their management headache of maintaining that building, and they receive a very strong financial benefit and public relations boost in the process. They convert their dead, nonperforming asset into vital cash, and, like in the rainforest, that process can be completed in as little as thirty days. The cost of acquisition for the foundation is minimal, which allows them to recycle the building back into usefulness by investing their savings into repair, rejuvenation, and getting it leased. The lease income funds the endowment.

Anytime you take an underperforming asset or something that has used up its useful life and break it down into the basic components, recombining them to make something new and useful that generates measurable and meaningful value, you have just fungigated. For seven years I was on the radio five days a week with a two-minute inspirational spot carried on about two hundred stations across America. The time came when the network with most of those two hundred stations decided to change their programming lineup, and I would have to change my organizational structure and content to stay onboard. We had a very friendly parting of ways. It was my opinion that the program in that format had served its purpose, and it was time for something else despite the tremendous popularity of that program.

I decided to fungigate. When you break it down, it was the message contained in the words that resonated with people. Not only was every broadcast recorded and on file, but so was the written transcript. We decided to offer those people a repackaged version of the very same messages but in the form of a daily coaching e-mail. Before long, there were hundreds, then thousands, and now tens of thousands of folks who subscribe to that free coaching program. You can too by going to www .SellingAmongWolves.com and registering for your free B-mail. It's interactive, so you can respond via the blog and dialogue with others with similar professional interests.

If the Internet were to go away, we could fungigate again by turning the best of them into a book with 365 of the all-time favorites bound together for a daily review on each day of the year. We could easily arrange them thematically and create a study course out of them or do a seminar. The possibilities are endless. There are an endless number of things that were popular at one time and have passed. They can be repackaged, redesigned, and repurposed with great result. If you have an eye for this, you may be a fungigator, a person who knows how to fungigate, and, as a specialist, bring in great revenues where others see only waste.

SIMPLIFYING THE COMPLEX

Another application of this truth is the ability to break down complex ideas or knowledge and put it in terms various market segments can understand easily and apply. Take, for example, this book. I spent tens of thousands of dollars traveling and researching the concepts I am laying out for you. I didn't do it with the idea I would create a wealth seminar or write a book. I simply did it to learn and apply that learning to my own business. The return on investment was more than worth it to me. The good news for you is that you don't have to spend $50,000 and several years to acquire the wisdom I received. That's why you bought this book, and if it resonates with you, you may want to join one of our Rainforest MasterMind groups for entrepreneurs and business leaders. (Check out www.RainforestStrategy.com for more information.)

When I traveled to the rainforest, I was given access to hundreds of scientific white papers written by Smithsonian scientists who had done years of research in various rainforests around the world. Their writings were fascinating and often used business vernacular, and there were a good number of words and concepts I had to look up in a dictionary! They weren't speaking my language, and I was not the intended reader. They were primarily communicating with other research scientists and using a lot of scientific terms. This book and our CD series called 7 Wealth Secrets of the Rainforest were a result of my decision to fungigate. I took the complex information that was unusable for the masses and broke it down into its fundamental components. I had to reformulate or restate complex concepts into simple terms and further translate them into common business language. It was a big project, but the result was that highly intellectual information of a complex nature was now accessible in simple terms that were immediately usable for any businessperson. This means you! Take what you learn in this book and be fruitful. Multiply. Thrive!

There are so many applications for this in business. Take wisdom that applies in one industry and repackage, redefine, and repurpose it for another. Years ago in the publishing industry, one of the leading book distributors made a deal with bookstores that if they would buy 90 percent of their inventory from them, they would receive highly favorable discounts and payment terms. They called it their 90/10 Plan. Bookstores were required to commit for at least a year, as I recall, and during that time the other distributors were pretty much locked out except for oddball orders here and there. The plan worked well in that industry.

Years later I was consulting for a company that supplied cutting tools to manufacturers. They sold things like drill bits to companies like Saturn. Their market penetration was shallow, and I suggested they fungigate. I didn't know the term at that time, but that's what it was. I took information (methodology from an unrelated industry—the 90/10 Plan) and broke it down into its basic components of increasing commitment on both ends for mutual benefit. We then drafted something virtually unknown in that industry, which we called a "Partner Program," where we offered a higher level of service, more favorable pricing, better terms, and faster delivery in exchange for the lion's share of their business. It was a powerful marketing proposition that worked, and it was basically fungigation.

One of my clients was a reputable, third-generation, privately owned local bank with multiple branches in a mid-size market. Their branch mangers would call on local businesses, introduce the bank, and discuss their checking account fees and savings account rates. The goal was to get the business owner to open an account and deposit their money with the bank. Having no prior experience in the banking industry, I had the advantage of a different perspective. I saw tremendous waste of effort, time, and message. I reasoned, What business owner got out of bed each day worried about where they would deposit their money? What business owner would seriously consider changing banks because they could save twenty dollars a month on their checking account service? And would you really want their business if they did?

When money is deposited in a bank, the bank immediately has a debt. They agree to pay you interest. If all they did was amass deposits, they would go broke. The profit is made in lending out the money on deposit on a leveraged (sometimes highly) basis.

Furthermore, growing businesses very often struggle with cash flow. They want to expand, build a new wing, add a new product line, open a new location, etc. They need cash for that. They get out of bed each day, not worried about where to deposit their money, but rather, where they can get their hands on more capital!

The bank was offering a place to deposit funds. The potential customers were looking for a place to get funds. There was a huge disconnect, and the resulting waste of time and talent screamed of an opportunity for fungigation! Remember, fungigation is the process of converting waste in any form to profit in any form. My job as a specialist was to recognize the waste and reformulate the message to lead with the pain the customers were having, positioning the bank as a valuable partner to the business community. They began the year hoping to match the previous record year in commercial loan volume. After the fungigation process, they experienced a 33 percent increase for the year! Considering it was the product with their highest profit potential, they were quite content.

Waste does not always mean that something has no value in its present form. It can simply be unrealized potential. That potential can often be tapped by emphasizing the right thing as in the bank example, or by simply giving an old thing a new name. The foundation I was helping struggled in the early years, running into resistance with corporate America due to strongly held, but quite inaccurate, perceptions about the transaction they proposed. It had gone by one name for so long that it meant something quite different in the mind of the business owner than what was in fact being offered by the foundation. As a result, they had a very difficult time getting to second base in the conversation because of these misconceptions.

There was no need to spend millions of dollars fighting an old, misguided perception. It was time to fungigate. The original transaction was renamed the "561 Exchange," which had no prior baggage in its meaning. The industry began researching the term based on Publication

561 of the IRS code and heralded it in publications like *Corporate Real Estate Leader* magazine as "the next revolution in corporate real estate."[16] Why has this phenomenon occurred? It's just like the banking example where the wrong thing was being emphasized, creating resistance and apathy. When the right thing was emphasized and, in this case, renamed to disassociate with the lingering misconception, the corporate doors swung wide open. Now a number of Fortune 500 Companies have done multiple million-dollar-plus transactions with the foundation, resulting in much needed economic stimulus, job creation, and a whole lot more!

Or consider this. I had recorded a teaching series called RainCatcher— 7 Ancient Paths to Wealth, Wisdom, and the Wonder of God. We added it to our online store, but for two years it got no traction. It was a great product with plenty of potential, but it was languishing on our shelves. For all intents and purposes, it was waste, lost profit. It needed fungigating. No product stands alone. Every product has a message, and sometimes the message we use to tell the story is the wrong message. Quite often the problem is not the product; it's the message you assign to the product. In this case we reformulated the message and married the new message to the old product, resulting in our highest unit sales that year for any CD series on our shelves.

Fungus simply takes discarded, organic product and turns it into profit that is used by the plant to produce useful product (biomass). Think of it as closed circuit teamwork to maximize profit. Leaves are what do the initial work: they receive and are energized by the vision (they are vision receptors); they take in the CO_2 (they add effort) and combine it with the water (information, know-how) to produce their product and more infrastructure. They release oxygen (reputation, goodwill) in exchange for carbon (hard work, effort). When a leaf can no longer serve the corporate vision, it falls away. Dead, organic matter on the forest floor speaks of vast amounts of untapped potential. Fungus closes the circle by getting a hold of that matter and repurposing it.

Sometimes the discarded leaf is a worker who gets laid off. It doesn't mean they have no purpose or meaning. It just means they need to quickly reintegrate into the workforce by repackaging themselves, reeducating themselves, or simply emphasizing their other underutilized skills. If you are leaf who has been let go from the corporate tree, find a specialist, a niche, a fungus who will help refocus and repurpose you to get back in the game. To speed up the process, imitate the rainforest model for high growth. Get a fresh vision for your future (light), find a source of encouragement (warmth), and soak up all the learning (water) you can to develop new skills, more value, and greater potential.

FUNGUS AS INTERNAL SPECIALIST

Fungus is one of countless specialists in the rainforest that make it absolutely thrive. In the rainforest, no one species dominates the landscapes, but rather you see an intricate web of interdependent relationships, cooperating and competing with each other. Adam Smith, in his foundational eighteenth-century book titled *An Inquiry into the Nature and Causes of the Wealth of Nations*, observed, "The greatest improvement in the productive powers of labor...seem[s] to be the effects of the division of labor."[17] The division of labor is nothing more than specialization, but he went on to point out "the extent of this division [of labor] must always be limited by...the extent of the market."[18] The simple reality is that the smaller the market, the smaller the productive potential of specialization.

To make his point, Smith examined a pin factory and compared the output of the factory using two different models. He concluded that if ten pin makers would each specialize on one unique step or function in the manufacturing process, those ten pin makers could produce forty-eight thousand pins per day. The very act of specializing helped each worker become more skillful, develop unique processes for their particular step, and avoid the loss of time associated with change-ups or refocusing on a different activity. When he compared the model of specialization in a pin factory with the model where each worker was responsible to make each pin from start to finish, he doubted they could output two hundred pins per day.

When Henry Ford came along to the automotive business, there were already over three hundred car companies, but he made the laws of specialization work for him. He created the assembly line and knocked just about everyone else out of business. The specialization allowed for skill improvement and, just like the pin factory, a much higher output.

The higher output created massive cost reductions, and the automobile came within reach of the average American for the first time. A specialist produces much more of a product, or part of a product, than they will ever consume on their own, but that is only productive if the excess ends up in the hands of those who value it.

This is in no way limited to manufacturing. One of the reasons for the astounding success of the foundation I assisted is the practice of specialization in their administrative and endowment-building practices. They build their endowment largely through the acquisition of underutilized or excess inventory of commercial real estate. When they began with their business model, one person would research available properties, create an offer, and follow it through. We gradually broke down the process to smaller steps, where there is now a department of specialists doing research, scouring the country for properties with the right profile from sellers with the right profile. They in turn pass over to another inside team of specialists the properties that appear to meet the criteria, who then contact the sellers by phone and further refine the opportunity.

If it looks promising, it is sent to yet another department that provides an in-house appraisal for estimation purposes, complete with comps and other valuation tools. If it meets the economic, physical, and geographic requirements of the foundation, they prepare an offer. Included with this offer is a comparison of their offer to a traditional offer with a chart showing the positive cash advantage of their unique 561 Exchange proposal. With this step now completed, a scheduler confirms with the seller that the offer has made it through the review process, and an appointment is scheduled for a face-to-face meeting with the owner. Another specialist called a RAM (regional acquisition manager), whose exclusive focus is presenting offers to qualified sellers, now enters the picture.

The foundation uses the laws of specialization to increase skill, increase output, and dramatically increase acquisitions. This process required an investment in personnel, but the result for the endowment has been a fivefold increase in value in a matter of months. Although that may sound impressive, the full benefit will not be realized before the end of 2008, because the specialists are just beginning to come together like a real team and learning how to best cooperate with each other.

EXTERNAL SPECIALIZATION

Specialists can be employed with great success internally in any process where demand for the output justifies the input. The same principles apply outward, and by being a specialist in the marketplace, there appears to be higher survival rates. The National Science Foundation reports on an amazing study done by thirty-three ecologists from twelve countries in seven undisturbed tropical rainforests. The big question they wanted an answer for was whether or not rare species (specialists) were rare because they were on the brink of local extinction, or because they were on their way to becoming more common. Their long-term study showed that there is indeed "an advantage to being rare, and that this advantage causes rare species to become more common."[19]

Researchers found that "the diversity of each local area increased regardless of the species that were present. This is because trees that were locally common tended to die more often than those that were locally rare, giving a survival advantage to rare species."[20] This held true even within a given species. "If a species was common in one part of a plot and rare in another, its death rate was higher where it was common."[21] They cite three likely reasons why specialists do so well.

1. **There are fewer pests and pathogens feeding on them when they are rare.**
Niche businesses tend to stay out of the crosshairs of predator companies. Niche businesses tend to keep a relatively low profile, except within their niche. A generalist doctor, for example, gets paid, but a specialist like a heart surgeon gets very well paid. They have less competition from their own field for resources.

2. **Specialists tend to share resources with other specialists with similar resource requirements.** Look at all the small business organizations that come together for group buying, group

lobbying, group support, and the like (NFIB, ICCC, Chamber of Commerce, NACFC, C12, AMA, FCCI, NSBA, CBN, and so on). Get with other specialists in your area or field and share resources.

③ Specialists tend to have a positive influence on others within their species because they are surrounded by a high proportion of trees that are different from themselves. Getting with other specialists is not just about resource sharing. You can share ideas, strategy, encouragement, and so on. It works for the rainforest, and it can work for you.

According to the National Council on Economic Education, "Specialization is a situation in which people produce a narrower range of goods and services than they consume, which increases productivity. Interdependence is a situation in which decisions made by one person affect decisions made by other people, or events in one sector of the economy affect other sectors of the economy. When people specialize, they do not try to provide for all their economic wants themselves; instead, for some wants, they depend on others. This is the basis of interdependence."[22]

The key to profiting from specialization outside of your business is finding a niche market with a growing base of readily accessible customers who can afford your product or service and are not particularly committed to a competitor of yours. Even the country's largest manufacturers target carefully pinpointed market segments to get the most out of their marketing dollars and out of their product or service. Focus on meeting their unique needs, communicated in their unique language or lingo. Don't try to market your products and services to everyone even if everyone needs it. Market to those who most need, want, and can afford your product. You will usually find them in smaller specialized groups or clusters. When you target smaller numbers of well-chosen market segments, your marketing budget goes further, and you have more to spend on each prospect to make the full impression and better communicate your message.

Focusing on the masses can be successful, but most of us can't afford to market successfully to a group that large. By trying to do so, we tend to limit our potential. Instead, focus on multiple niches, and in so doing, you connect with those people at a much higher level and quite naturally gain much more business. You end up with smaller target groups with much higher response rates and usually greater customer loyalty.

Take sales training, for example. Progressive companies routinely bring in outside consultants and/or trainers to develop their sales team. There are some industries with so many businesses in that industry that specialists gain a competitive advantage. A good sales trainer can adapt to any environment, but one who came out of the real estate industry with a highly successful track record will be more enthusiastically received and certainly better compensated if he or she specializes in real estate sales training. The same is true in auto sales. I didn't come from those backgrounds and chose instead to specialize in my content. The secret of my success came from the deliberate application of biblical principles and strategies to the sales process. For years I specialized in providing that content either covertly or openly to Fortune 100 companies and small businesses across America and in Canada, Central America, the Caribbean, and Europe. While not everyone shares my enthusiasm for the source of my materials, those who do put a very high value on it.

ACTION STEPS

1 If this book helps you at all, write out the three most important lessons you learned from it and share those lessons with someone else.

2 Identify at least three things you read that you know would help you if you applied them right away. Then put them in your calendar.

3 List three things that, if you fungigated them, could bring you a good return.

4 Think of one area in your business where specialization could bring you increase.

PRACTICE ABUNDANCE
Or Experience Scarcity

I came that they may have and enjoy life, and have it in abundance.[1]

JESUS CHRIST

Not everything that can be counted counts, and not everything that counts can be counted.[2]

ALBERT EINSTEIN

He who is plenteously provided for from within, needs but little from without.[3]

JOHANN WOLFGANG VON GOETHE

THE INESCAPABLE IMPRESSION ONE COMES AWAY FROM THE rainforest with is that of abundance. The riotous explosion of color and sound encapsulates you in a sea of green with more variety in an acre or two than in all of the United States and Canada combined! All of your senses are at once and immediately heightened as you try in vain to take it all in. Parades of leaf cutter ants cart off their haul of neatly cut leaf fragments, holding them high like miniature green sails catching the wind. Monkeys taunt and boast noisily in the canopy above, watching your every move. Birds of every color dart about policing the rainforest and spreading the word about any intruders. Bright blue butterflies dance in the subtle breeze as if celebrating a special day, while anteaters climb slowly up a tree looking for their favorite delicacy. Who needs a zoo? Just stand still in the rainforest and marvel at creatures great and small in every direction you look. None of them are suffering lack. Everywhere there is abundance.

Why on one hand do we embrace and gladly accept this visible display of abundance while on the other hand feel awkward or uncomfortable with the notion of abundance? Why is it that we see abundance in all of the created order, the fish of the sea, the stars in the sky, the birds of the air, the endless variations of sunrise and sunset, and the countless species of every kind, yet our minds are so full of limitations? Too many of us have been conditioned and trained not only to accept limits but also to self-impose those limits. When we were children, we thought we could fly through the sky or swim across the ocean. And if not us, then certainly our fathers could. If you could imagine it, then it was possible.

A scarcity mentality believes there is never enough to go around, what you do have won't last, and if there is abundance, it's a freak of nature, an abnormal condition. The result is a miserly, dare we say, miserable existence. Yes, there are limits in life. I acknowledge that, but too often we accept those limits as absolute. An abundance mentality sees limits as passports to abundance. They are entranceways to new and undiscovered sources of plenty. Take, for example, the supply of oil in the world. As we approach limits or "peak oil," where oil production begins to decline, there are a host of possibilities to slow down that trend. We can double or triple our fuel efficiency, and that effectively doubles or triples the supply. We can blend with ethanol to stretch it out. But let's say we actually run out of oil; do you really think we will go back to the horseless carriage? I think not. We will be forced to find an alternative as we approach real limits. Those alternatives will be an improvement along the lines of hydrogen, solar power, electric, or something even better.

A scarcity mentality only sees the limits while an abundance mentality sees the possibilities in spite of the limits. Thinking abundantly doesn't mean denying reality. It just means you have a firm conviction that reality can change for the better, that limits are temporal in nature, and that abundance is everywhere if you know where to look. Consider a simple piece of coal. One man sees it as a means to cook his next meal, while another just sees an object he can hurl at an opponent. We now know that with enough heat and pressure, that same piece of coal will become a diamond. In 1905, Einstein theorized that if somehow we could transform mass into energy, it would be possible to "liberate" huge amounts of energy.[4] He reportedly claimed there was enough atomic energy in a single piece of coal to power the *Queen Mary* ocean liner around the world! What you see depends a whole lot on what you are looking for. If you're looking for a stone to throw, any piece of coal will do. What you currently believe shapes and directs the things you are looking for so that you tend to find what you expect to see. If you don't like what you see, you probably need to change your thinking.

WHAT IMAGE DO YOU SEE?

It's as if there is an internal imaging/homing device that is constantly trying to locate or manifest in our life the image we see on the inside. If something doesn't match up with the image on the inside, we keep looking. If you see yourself as undeserving or unlovable, others will tend to see you that way as well. There's a story in the Bible where Moses sent out a reconnaissance team of twelve men to investigate the land of Canaan. They were to learn the lay of the land and the arable quality of the land, and size up the inhabitants. They came back with tales of giants and a land of plenty. Ten of them made an interesting statement, however, saying, "We were in our own sight as grasshoppers, and so we were in their sight."[5] In other words, they saw themselves as grasshoppers, and therefore the giants did too. They were looking for obstacles or reasons the new venture into the Promised Land wouldn't work.

Two of the men (Joshua and Caleb) had a different image on the inside. Looking at the same giants, they said, "They are bread for us!"[6] They were looking for provision and sustainability in the new land and saw the giants through a completely different grid. They saw them not as obstacles, but rather as a pathway to provision. These two fellows had a completely different picture of themselves than did the other ten. They saw themselves as victors and the giants as easy prey. Forty years later, when they finally entered the land, they found that the giants lived primarily on one of the mountains. Caleb, at the age of eighty, claimed dibs on the region controlled by the giants for himself! The land the giants controlled became provision for Caleb and his family for generations, while those who saw themselves as grasshoppers never made it back to the Promised Land.

If you don't like the image or result you see on the outside, change the image you see on the inside. When my firstborn daughter, Jennifer Lynn, was born with Down syndrome, I was devastated by the image I saw on the outside. All I had ever wanted was a healthy baby, but what I received was a handicapped child with a hole in her heart. I was young, very inexperienced at life, and emotionally devastated. I couldn't change her. I couldn't fix her. For no justifiable reason, the only thing I had ever feared would happen to me was that I would one day have a child with Down syndrome. The image I had on the inside became my reality on the outside.

I did something radical, and I did it the morning after I discovered her condition. (The doctors didn't tell us for over a week.) I reasoned that if a normal, healthy child on a scale of one to ten would be ranked a zero, incredibly gifted or talented children might be ranked a positive seven or eight. I carried this further and thought that if my daughter with less than normal abilities would be ranked by some at a minus eight, for example, then to me, I would view her as a positive eight. In other words, whatever number you attributed to her handicap in the negative column became the number on the positive side that I would see her. I changed my internal image of her, and while she never overcame her mental handicap, I certainly overcame mine! She was the most loving, accepting, and joyful human being I have ever met, and every day of her eighteen months on this planet was a deposit of something extraordinary in my life for which I have no regrets!

Sometimes you have to train yourself to see things differently on the inside, and that may involve some practical exercises. My wife is an accomplished artist and received a lot of help in learning to see things differently from a book called *Drawing on the Right Side of the Brain*. One of the exercises this book has you do is to sketch something like a photograph turned upside down. Because you are not familiar with how things are supposed to look upside down, you tend to more accurately sketch what is really there instead of what you think is supposed to be there.[7]

I suspect there's a correlation between left-brain thinking and seeing things as they are and right-brain thinking and seeing things as how they could be. Left-brain thinkers, it is claimed, tend to be more logical or rational, relying on historical information and empirical data. They tend to view life through the rearview mirror. Right-brain thinkers don't feel obligated to use logic because it may be flawed, or there may be a higher principle operating that we haven't yet discovered. They tend to drive down the road with their head out the window, ears flapping in the wind, wondering why everyone is staring at them! They generally don't like or don't accept limits. Left-brain-dominant people look for limits so they can make wise decisions based on that knowledge. Right brainers have never seen a box they can't get out of. Left brainers have never seen a box they can't live in. They use words and facts to describe concepts, whereas right-brain-dominant people tend to use pictures, illustrations, and relationships to describe a concept. Both are essential, and neither is to be ignored. That's why we have a whole brain.

I believe a profoundly important key to abundance, however, is the ability to tap into the power of right-brain thinking, the ability to see creatively what doesn't yet exist. Tap into this, and you have tapped into abundance. A left-brain person sees a block of marble and calculates its size, weight, and value, but a right-brain person like Michelangelo looks at a block of marble and sees the biblical figure David just waiting to be cut free from the limits of the marble block. As our society and world begin to approach limits in various forms, those who have learned to see with their right brain while harnessing the power and strength of the left brain will make this world a better place for everyone. While many will be worried about limits, they will be busy looking for the abundance that limitations birth. Just as necessity is the mother of invention, so are limits the breeding ground for abundance.

LEFT-BRAIN POWER

To better understand right-brain capacities, let's first take a look at some valuable left-brain tendencies. Knowing how to communicate with left-brain-dominant people is a critical skill regardless of your hemispheric orientation. Left-brain thinkers tend to think in a linear, straight-line, deductive process and rely heavily upon the following six communication styles:

L OGIC BASED

I NFORMATION CENTERED

N UMBERS ORIENTED

E VIDENCE FOCUSED

A NALYSIS WEIGHTED

R EFERENCE BALANCED

Logic

Left brainers are always trying to satisfy their intellect. Things have to be logical. Logic is something that can be demonstrated and replicated. It always holds true. It is reliable. Sir Isaac Watts wrote about logic in the 1700s and the power of logic to win arguments. His skills of reason and logic were taught in universities around the world. But logic by itself will never carry the day. There's an old saying, "A man convinced against his will is of the same opinion still." It's better to introduce logic after the heart has been won, then to try to persuade the heart using the head. Ninety percent of the decision is made in the heart, so why try to win an argument based on only 10 percent of the decision-making criteria? Win the heart first, which is the job of the right brain, and you can more easily satisfy the demands of the left brain.

Logic enables wisdom, and wisdom is of the highest value, so in no way do I wish to downplay the importance of left-brain tendencies of any sort. However, I believe they are best utilized when serving the pursuits of right-brain thinking. A left-brained person puts more weight on logic, so if you are a right brainer trying to convince a left brainer of something, you better have a sound, logical argument prepared.

Information

Augustine taught that logic was built on knowledge. Knowledge was the accumulation of facts, but logic was the ability to connect the dots and make a wise deduction. Your logic is only as good as the information you provide. In rainforest vernacular, water is information. Left-brained people can never get enough information. They love to learn and acquire knowledge, which is another great trait of left-brain-dominant people. Knowledge is power in reserve. Logic knows how to best use knowledge, but timing is left up to the heart. If you want to impress a left-brained person, you better know what you are talking about or you will quickly lose them.

I am an advocate of whole-brain living, so even though I tend to be more right brained than left, I wholeheartedly support the pursuit of knowledge or information. It serves the right brain in that it opens it up to possibilities previously unknown to you. Strengthen this capacity by becoming an expert in your field. Read a book a week for a year on your topic of interest, and you will become a national expert by most standards. In three years, you'll be considered an international expert.

Numbers

Another form of information, numbers are powerful because everyone knows "numbers don't lie." In business you had better know and watch the numbers more closely than you do the stories that come with those numbers. In the end, the bank wants a number, not a story; the investors want a number (ROI), not a story; and if right brainers have a weakness (and they have many), it would be their propensity for coming up with stories to explain away the numbers.

A CEO friend of mine once told me that he just wanted to see the numbers because the numbers tell the real story. If you ask a sales rep to explain their numbers, you may well get quite a different story than the numbers themselves tell. Yes, there's always a human story to tell, but left-brained people don't want to hear the sob story; they just want the facts. They prefer to be objective, not subjective. They may not see very far in the future, but they are pretty accurate at seeing what the present moment looks like.

Evidence

Evidence is not always proof in the mind of the skeptic. Therefore it's a good idea when trying to convince a left brainer of your right-brained concept to have multiple forms of evidence to offer. When it comes to validating your claims, be exact. Inexact numbers don't carry much weight as evidence, but exact numbers do. If you must use estimations, have them make the estimation so they buy into the result. Here are several different forms of evidence a left brainer might accept:

E XHIBITS (WORKING MODEL, PHYSICAL SAMPLE, ETC.)

V ALIDATING WRITTEN REFERRALS (RESPECTED TESTIMONIALS FROM PEERS)

I NDEPENDENT STUDIES (RESPECTED PUBLICATIONS)

D EMONSTRATION (SHOW THEM HOW IT WORKS)

E XAMPLES (RELEVANT ILLUSTRATIONS OF OTHERS WHO HAVE MADE THE SAME DECISION)

N EWS REPORTS (RESPECTED PUBLICATIONS)

C ASE HISTORIES (DETAILED, FACTUAL STORIES PRESENTED IN A CASE STUDY FORMAT)

E XPERT OPINION (RESPECTED TESTIMONIAL)

Analysis

The left side of the brain loves to analyze things. Help your left-brained friends and customers process the information by analyzing it with them. "Ted, let's analyze this together and see if it makes sense to you." Providing written analysis from others who have taken your advice, purchased your product, or followed your example will go a long way to convincing left-brained people to follow suit.

References

Generally speaking, people don't want to be the guinea pig. They need to know that others have gone on before and been glad they did. The higher the profile of these references and the more specific they are to the conversation at hand, the more powerful the reference. Secure a plethora of reference letters and case histories of your business successes, and distribute them freely to prospective clients.

In one study I read, an advertiser sent out a promotion with a page of referral quotes and received a good response. Out of curiosity, he mailed out the same ad to a similar list but with two pages of referral quotes. His response rate increased. He did it again with four pages, then eight pages, then sixteen, then thirty-two, then sixty-four. Surprisingly, each subsequent mailing increased the response rate, and the only difference was the body of reference quotes. The last time I checked, he was putting together a book of referral quotes to include in his mailer. The increased response rate wasn't dramatic, but it was consistently higher when he included more reference quotes from satisfied customers. As you build your business, build your library of testimonial letters of reference to help prospects justify what they know in their heart they already want to do.

Now to the fun part…my world…

RIGHT-BRAIN THINKING

Right-brain thinking has seven key traits or means of expression. They are best suited to win the heart, the emotional side of the sale. Right-brain concepts allow us to easily differentiate from the others, to stand out from the crowd and be noticed. The left-brain traits satisfy the intellect, but the right brain woos the heart and can rapidly speed up the transaction. For example, a left-brain person who wants to find a mate will put together a checklist of desirable traits. When he or she meets a person who has those traits, the left brainer analyzes, evaluates, and typically procrastinates with drawn-out engagements after lengthy dating periods. Introduce that same left-brained person to the one who captures his or her heart, the one whose presence makes every grain of sand sparkle like a diamond, every color brighter, and every sound a fine-tuned instrument in the symphony of life, and they will be married before the weekend is over!

You may well want to win the argument, settle the dispute, and win your case, but first win the heart, the nonlinear, intangible, hard-to-measure but irresponsible-to-neglect part of the human psyche. In the rainforest, the only straight lines you see are tree trunks reaching for the light (vision). Everything else is a tangled web of seemingly random parts making a whole that functions better as a system than anything man has ever attempted to create. It's right brain gone to seed with left brain encoded in the DNA still waiting to be discovered. What we see is a feast for the right brain. How it works is an endless banquet for the left brain. Here's how the right brain speaks:

H EIGHT: GIVES A GLOBAL PERSPECTIVE; SHOWS THE BIG PICTURE

I LLUSTRATION: CREATES UNDERSTANDING; TRANS-LATES INTO THEIR LANGUAGE

S TORY: GIVES MEANING; MULTIPLIES PERCEIVED OR EMOTIONAL VALUE

P ASSION: AMPLIFIES THAT PERCEIVED VALUE

E MPATHY: OPENS THE DOOR TO HEAR YOUR MESSAGE

E XPERIENCE: ENGAGES THE SENSES

D ESIGN: ADDS VALUE

Height

Fly above the rainforest, and you begin to get a glimpse of how vast it is in places, how utterly and completely full it is, brimming with life at every level. There are five layers or levels in the rainforest, each with their distinct plant species, animal life, and climate. The "emergent" level has the tallest trees that have emerged above the level of the other trees in the forest to form umbrella-shaped canopies with heights up to two hundred feet. In business these would be the Fortune 500 companies, the undisputed leaders in their field with household names.

Following that is the "upper canopy" at about one hundred feet, with lots of light and lots of food, supporting lots of animal life. In fact, there is so much food at this level that some animals never go down to the forest floor. In business, these would be the myriad of well-established successful corporations that feed so many. They have lots of vision and provide lots of value to many. This is followed by the "understory" at the sixty-foot level, consisting of trunks of canopy trees and generally smaller trees. To me, this speaks of the support industries that make the bigger companies successful. It's the company you've never heard of in a place like McMinnville, Tennessee, that manufactures steering wheels for a car company.

Then you have the fourth layer, the "shrub/sapling" layer maxing out at thirty feet, characterized by the amount of stunted growth due to lack of light (vision). They are capable of a rapid growth surge when a gap in the canopy opens up above them. This speaks to me of the countless smaller companies with small or greatly diffused vision who nonetheless carry great potential in their DNA. When their vision is expanded, they will grow exponentially.

Lastly, you have the forest floor, which receives only 1–2 percent of the sunlight. It is so starved for light that very little grows there at all, making it easy to walk through most parts of the forest floor. Moisture content is also greatly reduced, since about one-third of the precipitation is intercepted by the canopy above. This speaks to me of start-ups with little vision (light), minimal information (water), and little chance of success. Unlike a tree, however, these folks can reposition themselves to be exposed to great vision and lots of information and become the tree they were always meant to be.

The left brain sees the individual levels of the rainforest, but only for what they are. The right brain sees them in another context as well as the integrated whole. It's about the big picture. It's about being visionary, seeing what's possible, crossing boundaries, understanding metaphors, and seeing patterns. It's more about strategy than the tactical. To give "height" to your interaction, take the conversation beyond the transaction and into what it will mean for them when the transaction is completed. The transaction is tactical. The long-term effect is strategic. Suppose you sell pianos. If you want to give height to your presentation, introduce the parent to the long-term, large-scale benefits, one of which is enhanced intellectual capacity. It's a well-known fact that playing a musical instrument, especially the piano, increases your brainpower. The music is nice, but the payoff has far-reaching consequences and may set a person up for life because of their higher academic achievement.

Because height adds value, it increases abundance. Bring a global, fifty-thousand-foot perspective to what you are offering, and you increase the potential reward for everyone involved. Give your employees a global perspective, and you will have more buy-in to the vision. Give your customers a global perspective, and they will invest more heavily with you. Watch any television commercial for financial services, and they will give you a global, long-range perspective about your grandchildren's education or your golden retirement years really being golden. The better they are at getting you to see the big picture, the more likely you will be to invest. What's the big picture you offer your customers? Are you communicating that?

Illustration

An illustration creates a visual picture in the mind using accepted relationships that cause understanding and lead to action. It's not so much a story as it is a vignette. People refer to the glass being half full or half empty as an accepted illustration for optimism vs. pessimism. That's an illustration. Years ago a client of mine, Centurion Technologies out of St. Louis, pioneered a technology for use in computer classes at public schools. As they explained it to me, the kids in class sometimes thought it was their assignment to crash the school computers or, better yet, the entire system so they would get to have some free time. Their technology enabled Windows and Macintosh platform users to explore, experiment, and make mistakes without penalty or permanency. The technology not only protected computers from user error or malicious intent, but it also protected them from the very real dangers of spyware, viruses, Trojans, and other harmful downloaded programs. With their technology in your computer, all you have to do to deal with bad stuff your computer may have picked up is to reboot, restore, and rejoice! You couldn't defeat their software, which has made it a favorite in school districts and libraries across the country.

This was a new concept to a lot of computer lab teachers and school board members, so to make it easy to understand, we used an illustration. We asked them to envision a large classroom with clean, white walls full of kids who have just been handed Magic Markers. An hour later, there is graffiti on the walls and ink spots everywhere; the room is a mess. Imagine if all you had to do when the students left the room was to turn the light switch off and then turn it back on again, and the room would be back in its original condition—white, clean, and orderly. That's what the proposed software would do for them! People understood that illustration better than they often did the technical, left-brain explanation about virus protection and restoring bios, etc., etc. You want to make the benefits of your product or service so easy to understand that a caveman would get it!

Illustration connects people to the value you bring. Take some time and develop one or two really good illustrations that vividly and clearly demonstrate the value of each of the key features of your product or service. Illustration increases value perception, which in turn releases valuable resources, which in turn creates abundance. Don't just read this point and move on. Consider every important thing you must communicate in your business environment, and find a reliable, easy-to-understand, authoritative illustration that makes the point. Then use it!

A friend of mine was in the mobile billboard business. He had moving billboards that rotated every sixty seconds on every side of a specially designed truck, and he drove through traffic, attracting much attention. You would think it would be easy to sell advertising space, but he was having difficulty making inroads because traditional advertisers didn't know how to value it. I suggested he get a dozen coffee beans and one Mexican jumping bean and put them all on the desk of a traditional, stationery billboard advertiser and begin his presentation while ignoring the beans. Obviously the Mexican jumping bean would keep grabbing the advertiser's attention while all the others lay motionless. Then he was to simply ask the advertiser which bean caught his attention. Of course, it would be the one moving around his desk. Then he was to simply tell the advertiser, "That's what this is!" and then explain that most people ignore billboards, but a moving billboard with rotating messages is unavoidable: "You have to look, just as you looked at the moving bean on your desk!"

Story

As long as there have been people, there have been stories. No culture in the world lacks a story of their history. Before they discovered fire, they had a story. Mind you, it got better when they discovered fire, which also became the gathering place to tell stories. According to cognitive scientist Robert C. Schank, "Humans are not ideally set up to understand logic; they are ideally set up to understand stories."[8] And in his book *Things That Make Us Smart*, Donald Norman claims, "Stories have the felicitous capacity of capturing exactly those elements that formal decision-making methods leave out. Logic tries to generalize, to strip the decision making from the specific context, to remove it from subjective emotions. Stories capture the context, capture the emotions.... Stories...encapsulate, into one compact package, information, knowledge, context, and emotion."[9]

The purpose of "story" is to engage the emotions, arouse the imagination, and capture the heart. The facts can then be used to support or justify the desire that has been created. Dan Pink (no relation), in another of his insightful books, says, "3M gives its top executives storytelling lessons. NASA has begun using storytelling in its knowledge management initiatives. And Xerox—recognizing that its repair personnel learned to fix machines by trading stories rather than by reading manuals—has collected its stories into a database called Eureka that Fortune estimates is worth $100 million to the company."[10]

Don't underestimate the power of "story." Use it wisely and truthfully to your advantage. While much of your competition spins masterful webs of logic, squandering precious face time with prospects by appealing to the wrong side of the brain, you can use both sides of your brain in the proper sequence and carry the day!

Story has the potential to greatly enhance value perception. What is value anyway if it is not perception? Isn't beauty in the eye of the beholder? So must value also be at the discretion of the customer. You set the price, but the customer determines the value. Because value in many ways is so subjective, you should use every form of subjective communication to develop your value message. How much is freedom worth? What is the price of freedom? If you were imprisoned in Algiers, how much would you pay for your freedom? Would you measure it in terms of lost revenue for every day spent in prison? I don't think so. While I can't verify the veracity of this story, I was told of a lawyer who defended people wrongfully charged with murder. His price? Everything you owned. Everything. But he would get you off, and his clients considered it a fair trade. Wouldn't you?

So let's talk about "story" a little. One of my favorite restaurants in the world was a Tex-Mex place in Nashville called Texana. They had the best smoked chicken quesadillas anywhere! On the back of their menu they had the most compelling story of their history and a high school football game that made the record books. Just reading their story made you want to buy shares in the restaurant. When they got tired of being in the restaurant business, they closed up and went back to Texas, but while they were open, they were always in high demand. The Tex-Mex restaurant that moved in after them was a chain restaurant with good food but no story, and they never did as well as the original.

Story has the power to bind the listener (customer) to the seller with bands of loyalty that defy logic. Increased loyalty means increased revenue, which is another way you increase abundance using right-brain strategies. Use your right brain for generating profits and your left brain for counting them! When I was a child, we lived for a time in a very small town in a grand old Victorian-era house. Years later I went back to visit my childhood home, and the owner graciously allowed me in. While I was visiting, he brought out an old dusty violin he said he found under the staircase when he bought the house from my parents. It didn't look like much, but he seemed pretty proud of it. How much was that secondhand violin worth, do you suppose? Not too much.

But what if I told you the violin was made by Antonio Stradivarius in 1707? That it was made for his only daughter Christina to be played at her wedding, a wedding that his wife, whom he loved more than life, would not attend because she died giving birth to Christina? Imagine Antonio raising his daughter and telling her as she grew up all about her mother so she would have some fragmented way of knowing her. Imagine the love he would put into making this violin so late in his life. Imagine the dedication and commitment to quality of materials and workmanship.

Then imagine the sound of this magnificent violin as it played the wedding march and other pieces at Christina's wedding. Don't just imagine it; what if I could show you the violin and let you play it and actually hear the incandescent sound that comes from mastery?

Then what if I told you, that violin now called Christina's Hammer was the last violin Antonio ever made, because three days after his daughter's wedding, he died with a smile of total fulfillment on his face and an expectancy in his heart to reunite with his wife again?

Now, how much is that violin worth? If you said millions, you are probably right. The story I just told was fictional, but on May 16, 2006, a Stradivarius violin known as the Christian Hammer, made in 1701, was sold for $3,544,000. You can bet there's quite a story associated with that one—and that someone liked the story enough to put a value of millions of dollars on it. That's the power of story. Use it wisely, frequently, confidently, and truthfully, and you will be well rewarded, experiencing increased abundance in the process.

Passion

It's the presence of conviction about what you are doing, what you are saying, and what you are representing. Many a jury has been persuaded by the passion of the trial lawyer. Augustine of Hippo called it rhetoric. It's the ability to communicate in a way that stirs the emotions. You have to find the passion for yourself before you can ignite it in others.

Selling, at its base level, is merely the transference of passion. If you are not passionate about what you are doing, find something else. Passion creates abundance. It ramps up the value in the heart of the customer. Like all right-brain strategies, passion can be misused to inflame people to make rash decisions they will later regret. Don't do that. Just because you shouldn't beat up strangers with a bat doesn't mean you shouldn't play baseball!

Another word for passion might be enthusIASM, the last four letters of which stand for "I Am Sold Myself." Passion comes from knowing, not guessing or speculating, but knowing with certainty what your product or service can and cannot do for someone. If you do not know with certainty, how can you expect your customers to know? Passion moves people. Logic justifies the move. Many a passionate man or woman has bid up the price well beyond reason in an auction.

Empathy

It's not feeling bad "for" someone. That's sympathy. This is about feeling "with" that person, sensing what it would be like to actually be that person. It's the ultimate virtual reality, climbing into someone else's psyche to experience their grief, pain, or joy from their perspective. It involves not only giving meaningful feedback in the conversation but also having the vocal tones, body language, and sense of timing to match. I read about a pastor who went over to the home of one of his church members who had just lost their son in a tragic accident. He felt horrible because he didn't know what to say. He just sat with them and wept with them. That was empathy. They didn't need answers. They needed love.

In business, being able to empathize with people who are in some kind of pain increases your value to them. I remember when I was doing some training for a management consulting firm. My first job was to travel with one of their salesmen and see where I could bring improvement. This guy's strategy for sales was to suit up, show up, and throw up! He asked no questions, developed no rapport, and cared nothing for the customer. He just showed up, spewed out his presentation, and went for the close. He was rude, dishonest, and quite pathetic, but the company he worked for was reputable, and they wanted my assessment of him.

On this particular call after five straight closing attempts, the business owner got up to physically remove the both of us from his office. He was red-faced and very ticked off! The sad part was that the service being offered was ideal for him, but the salesman had broken the golden rule in trust building. He lied. He coerced. He manipulated. He lost the sale! I was in pain watching this ordeal unfold in front of me and finally felt compelled to speak up, though I was not well versed on the service being offered.

The first thing I did was empathize with the owner. I explained that I was not really with that company, but rather a consultant brought in to help them improve their service. I told him that, from my perspective, there was nothing that salesman said that had any value to him. He was surprised and agreed. I told him that I wouldn't buy based on the information he had either. He was beginning to like me. I spoke truthfully, asked some piercing questions, continued empathizing with him, then restated the offer in precise and *accurate* terms, and then gave him the opportunity to accept the offer, which, if implemented, would significantly impact his business in a positive manner. What he heard made sense to him, and it was spoken with compassion, empathy, and truth. This time he bought! Empathy changed the dynamic, increased the receptivity, and carried the day. Without doubt, empathy has the potential to increase value and thereby abundance.

Experience

This is about engaging the whole person, not just the intellect. What can you show them? Can you meet with them? How about a visit to their office? Get them involved with you and in the whole process. The more "clinical," "sterile," and "official" you keep the process, the less engaged the prospect will be, and the less likely you will be to have a successful conclusion.

I read once that people were 35 percent more likely to buy a product in the grocery store if they touched it. Charmin toilet paper took full advantage of that truth and enjoyed great success. When IBM introduced the desktop computer to the office environment, I read that 88 percent of the sales were made by just 11 percent of the sales force. The differentiating factor was that the 11 percent of the sales force went to the trouble of physically bringing the computer to customers' offices to let them enter the key strokes and experience the computer.

One of my early mentors in life, to whom I owe a debt of gratitude, is a man by the name of Gerry Price. Back in the late 1960s, he sold Xerox copiers in the then lightly populated area known as the Fraser Valley in British Columbia. He wanted his prospects to experience Xerography, which was not in common use at the time. He purchased a motor home, converted it to an office on wheels, loaded it up with the most popular copiers, and brought them to the prospect's office for a demonstration. He would engage and involve them in the demonstration, allowing them to make the copies and participate in the process. That year, he won salesman of the year for Xerox of Canada despite having what most would consider a backward territory!

Find a way to let your customers experience your product, service, or ideas. When you do, you will have added value, and that increases abundance.

Design

It's the combination of function and significance. It's function, enhanced by significance. Making a sale has a very utilitarian aspect to it. We make a contact, determine needs, propose a solution, and sign a contract. Then do it again. That's the function. Think of coffee. You pour hot water over ground coffee beans. Not hard to do, yet millions of people pay top dollar to hire Starbucks to make their coffee for them. Why Starbucks over McDonalds? McDonalds serves coffee. Starbucks serves up ambience, experience, story, and passion. They offer physical beauty, and the experience is emotionally compelling. (Don't believe me? Watch the reaction when you give someone a Starbucks gift card!) They design the entire purchase to be memorable.

Remember the Stradivarius violin? It used to be a block of rough-hewn wood. Then someone, a master, added design, and it went from a commodity to a rarity—a thing of beauty and excellence. What did shape or design have to do with value? It's all in the eye and the heart of the customer. The aging of the wood, the choice of the maple and the spruce, and the selection of the strings all go into making that instrument release its signature sound to resonate gently with our soul, calling us to something higher that we don't fully understand and never completely forget. That is the power of design.

Buy a lump of clay for forty cents a pound. Add the right design, and sell it for four dollars an ounce. But it's not just material objects that appreciate in value when you add design. You can add design to a wedding, a meal, a customer experience of any kind. You can affect their sense of sight, smell, and sheer delight by something as simple as design. Gone are the days where design merely improved function. Now, design is about adding value, prestige, confidence, comfort, and ambience. Robert Lutz, vice chairman of General Motors, when speaking about GM and the auto business in general, said a most intriguing thing: "It's more right brain....I see us being in the art business. Art, entertainment, and mobile sculpture, which coincidentally, also happens to provide transportation."[11]

Practicing abundance is as simple as flowing with the genius and generosity of your right brain. It will create more opportunities for abundance than you will ever be able to act upon. As was aptly stated in Mark Victor Hansen and Robert Allen's book, *The One Minute Millionaire*, "There is an ocean of abundance, and one can tap into it with a teaspoon, a bucket, or a tractor trailer. The ocean doesn't care."[12] Practice the principles of abundance this week. Use your brain. Yes, my friend—both sides!

ACTION STEPS

1 In what ways do you demonstrate a scarcity mentality, if any?

2 What will you do to counter that mentality?

3 On a separate piece of paper, list the most important features of the product or service you represent. Beside each, identify the best left brain (LINEAR) and right brain (HI SPEED) examples to help communicate the benefit of those features clearly and convincingly.

WEALTH SECRET #2:

GROW TOWARD THE LIGHT
Powered by Vision

Where there is no vision, the people perish.[1]

SOLOMON

Vision gives pain a purpose.[2]

KRIS VALLOTTON

O NE OF THE MAGNIFICENT THINGS ABOUT THE RAINFOREST that you are struck with immediately is that everything, I mean everything, grows toward the light. The simple rule in the jungle is, "He with the most light grows the fastest and becomes the biggest." Plants, of course, are limited by their type, but two plants of the same species with unequal light access will have quite different outcomes in their growth. When a gap opens in the canopy due to a fallen tree, for example, a previously stunted tree is quite capable of a rapid growth surge.

Because light provides the energy to manufacture food for the plant, competition in the rainforest for that light is fierce, and very little light, less than 2 percent, actually reaches the ground. Leaves are shaped and positioned to maximize light absorption depending on where they are in the forest, and trees will spend more to place their leaves in the light than to make them in the first place.

So what does this all mean in the context of business? Well, at a very fundamental level, light enables vision. Without light, we would have no vision. When we consider the rainforest as a business model, I believe we must consider light as being analogous to vision. Vision provides clarity. Clarity allows focus. Focus gives certainty. Certainty encourages action. Action produces results. Results are how we are measured. Measurement shows where to improve.

Rainforest trees depend on fresh light every day—not some of the time, not just in summer, but every day. It fuels them. It drives them. It grows them! As a result, they seek it daily. A company or an individual without a vision is, at best, a seed blowing in the wind. It may go places, but it will never amount to anything until it's planted and starts seeking the light! Significant accomplishment is always the product of significant vision.

Oftentimes, our vision is obscured by other people or things that line up endlessly to get our attention. With no ill intention, they block the light, and unless we deliberately and decisively cut away and put aside that which divides our attention, we will lose precious light. Think of light as the electricity that powers the rainforest, and when that power is diminished, everything moves much slower or not at all.

Like light, vision is the power that drives purposeful activity. If you're not getting much done, or if your vision seems a long way off, you may be suffering from "vision interruptus," a condition of frustration that occurs when you're always busy but not getting any closer to the fulfillment of that vision. My good friend Eric Beck states, "An analogy I use in human combat is that if you can even slightly damage your opponent's eyes, you can invalidate up to 95 percent of his strength. Two ounces of pressure applied to the opponent's eyes in a quick backhand strike beats 600 pounds of power. Not a bad deal considering ROI."

WHY PEOPLE OFTEN DON'T FULFILL THEIR VISION

Vision is an inner knowing of exactly what you are doing and why. It sees the result and can communicate its value to others. Vision is about seeing, having a sense of direction, and knowing where you want to end up. A lot of people have a vision of what they want to do and who they want to become, but they never get there. Ever wonder why? There are many reasons, but among the principle ones is the fact that they don't know their starting point. I have a GPS system in my car. It is not an option. For me, it is a necessity! I can easily get lost and have been known to stop for gas on a long trip, and then get back on the interstate heading the wrong way! For the GPS system to work best, it must first know where you are NOW. What is your starting point? It is only from there that the directions and vision make sense.

I've seen contestants on *American Idol* with a firm conviction they were the next American Idol. The worthiness of that goal or lack thereof notwithstanding, the contestant did not have a clear vision of who they were, what talents they truly possessed, what they were really wired for, and so on. As a result, they were not ready for the competition, would not prepare themselves for it, and will therefore never achieve it. Vision begins with seeing yourself clearly. It is only from a right understanding of who you are, how you are wired, what moves you deeply, and why that you will develop a clear starting point from which to navigate yourself toward your dream. Too often, however, people set their sights on a goal, a destination, without first having an accurate understanding of their starting point.

If we don't accurately and realistically and certainly enter in the correct starting point, and if we insist on a starting point that is not where we really are, we are headed for serious trouble. It's not necessarily the vision or destination point that we need to change; it may just be the starting coordinates. Taking an honest assessment of yourself in no way suggests that you have to remain at that place, but you can't correct what you won't acknowledge. People who are too afraid to acknowledge the truth about themselves will lie about any number of other things too. As Shakespeare once said, "To thine own self be true." If you won't be true to yourself, the rest doesn't matter.

So let's get started on this vision quest.

1. See yourself clearly.

Admit your weaknesses. Acknowledge your failings. Don't wallow in them or get stuck in self-pity. Discern the causes. Make amends where possible. Don't overestimate yourself. Don't underestimate what God can do through you. Get clear on your strengths. Ask true friends to tell you what they see in you, both the good and the bad. If they don't love you enough to tell you the truth, make some friends who will.

By the way, having a weakness doesn't necessarily preclude you from a specific vision. You just have to have other compensating factors. Conventional wisdom says you have to be tall to play basketball in the NBA, but Earl Boykins, formerly with the Denver Nuggets, didn't get that memo. He's five-foot-five and is the smallest man in the NBA. Being small never stopped him from coming up big for the Denver Nuggets as much as, if not more than, anyone on the team. He also holds the record for the most points scored in overtime by any player in the NBA.[3] While it didn't look like Boykins was designed for basketball, he alone saw the blueprint on the inside and compensated the height deficiency with speed and the heart of a lion!

2. Look for the design.

An acorn is the creation of the oak tree, and when it is planted, we all know where it's headed. The acorn need only look to its Creator to understand what it was created to be. While I believe we have more options available to us than the mighty oak, we would still be wise to seek the Creator to discover what we are here to do on this earth. We are more than a random collection of cells. We have a design, and design speaks of purpose and infers there is a Designer, but when design is not known, the Designer is not recognized. When we don't know the design, we can't know the purpose. Where purpose is not known, abuse is inevitable. The Beverly Hillbillies used a pool table for their dining table and its pockets for cup holders. Purpose was not known, so abuse was inevitable.

Maybe you think you have no special talent upon which to build, but every plant in the rainforest has a special design and purpose, and so do you. Not one was made without a unique purpose. Just because you don't know your special design or purpose doesn't mean there isn't one. The reason so many people don't see or recognize their gifting is because they don't work for it. It comes natural to them. What comes naturally to you that other people struggle with? That's a clue to one of your many gifts. Years ago my wife and I wrote a series of books compiling Scripture together in conversational format addressing a myriad of business and life situations. I thought it was so easy a caveman could do it. The books sold hundreds of thousands of copies. When we contracted with others to create some of the new books we had envisioned but lacked the time to write, we were sorely disappointed. What was easy to us was difficult and cumbersome to them. We had a gift and didn't know it. A gift or talent is so easily missed precisely because we don't have to work for it. It's a gift!

3. Find the gold.

There are also latent gifts and talents lying beneath the surface of our personality just waiting to be discovered. In many respects we are like a gold mine. Sure, there's a lot of dirt, rock, and clay, but there is also gold. On the surface all we see is the dirt, but make no mistake, there is gold within. We were made in the likeness of God, and as the saying goes, "God don't make no junk!"

People tend to look at the blemishes on the surface and miss the deposit of gold buried within. Everyone has a vein of gold running through them—everyone! It's just that some people don't want to get a shovel and do the hard work of pulling it to the surface. They believe what others tell them about themselves. They only see the outside, but the true value is buried like treasure on the inside. In fact, it's the gold buried within that is our true identity, our reflection of the image of God. We all have a piece or a portion of that reflection. None of us have it all, but all of us have some. We must mine it and refine it. That's another way of saying we must discover our gifting and develop it. Sometimes that can happen in unexpected ways.

When my wife's nineteen-year-old son was killed in a car wreck, she took up oil painting as a form of therapy. The pain of her loss cut deep, but it revealed a vein of gold previously unknown. Now her art reflects the profound work of grace etched upon her soul in a way that brings life and joy to others. That being said, she still had to diligently apply herself to this gift, developing and refining it over the years, finally ending up with polished gold set in places of honor.

4. Find out what moves you.

What stirs passion in you? What truly matters to you? It contains the clues to your spiritual DNA and the problems you can help solve in the world. Do an inventory of the things that flow naturally with your talents. Look at what life has prepared you for so far. Use your mistakes as stepping-stones and learn from them. The more they cost you, the more value they have. Don't pay the price and not take home the prize.

When you are clear on who you really are and that you were designed with purpose, when you know your strengths and weaknesses and what really moves you at the core, you have pegged your starting point of your GPS and are ready to plug in the coordinates of the desired destination. You are ready to create or define your vision. There's the vision for your family, perhaps a different one for your business, and yet another one for your personal development, and so on. If you are going to take the time to define a vision for your business, be sure to define one for the other spheres of your life. I define the seven spheres as follows.

1 **Work.** This represents our vocational lives, what we want to accomplish with our labor. It's our business, our entrepreneurial passion, the thing we build so we can realize our vision in the other spheres. This is the one we will spend time developing in this book.

2 **Others.** This is about the relationships that matter most to us—our family, friends, peers, and so on. If we only define a vision for our work life and don't plan for relationships, we may end up being rich and lonely. The vision may include being married, having children, or simply defining the quality of relationship you want to have with those important to you. It's less about who and more about the description of what that relationship looks like.

3 **Resources.** I am speaking of tangible, measurable goals that you can envision. These may include a certain standard of living, income levels, financial security, and the like. I kind of like what Forrest Gump said after selling Bubba Gump Shrimp, "And so then I got a call from him saying we don't have to worry about money no more. And I said, 'That's good. One less thing.'"[4] Resources are important, but as Forrest Gump's momma once said, "There's only so much fortune a man really needs."[5]

4 **Spiritual.** We all have a spiritual side to us. Some of us explore it, and others don't. Some even deny it, but that doesn't change the fact that there is a spiritual craving inside of us that longs for expression and fulfillment. Find the truth, and don't settle for counterfeits. Remember the ASK principle:

> **A** SK AND IT WILL BE GIVEN.
>
> **S** EEK AND YOU WILL FIND.
>
> **K** NOCK AND IT WILL BE OPENED.

5 **Health.** This one is easy to ignore when you are healthy and impossible to miss when you're not. Develop a vision for your wellness. Remember that discipline is the fruit of vision. When you don't have discipline in your diet or exercise, it is likely a result of not having a compelling vision for that part of your life.

6 **Intellectual.** If you think education is expensive, try being ignorant! Consider goals that challenge your mind, like learning another language, reading a book for an hour a day, listening to inspirational CDs, reading autobiographies of successful people, studying history, or watching the Discovery Channel. A mind truly is a terrible thing to waste.

7 **Personal.** Life should not be all work and no play. Get a vision for some recreation, rejuvenation, and reward for accomplishment. Maybe take up horseback riding, water skiing, or just frequent trips to a cabin in the woods. The object here is to get a vision for your personal life, where you can get recharged, refreshed, and renewed.

Vision is defined as "the ability to perceive something not actually visible, as through mental acuteness and keen foresight."[6] Your vision for any of these spheres should have clear-cut objectives and a sound plan of action, be guided by values, be supported by wisdom, and be executed from your strengths with faithfulness. A strategic vision provides direction, guidance, and motivation. If you are not clear on where you are going, why should anyone follow you? If you are clear on this, you must communicate this to other stakeholders or they cannot follow you.

Remember that trees spend more of their resources positioning their leaves in light (vision) than they do in making them. The lesson is simple: you should invest more in making sure other team members are continuously exposed to the vision than you would in recruiting and hiring them in the first place. The recruitment process is important, but keeping the team constantly exposed to the vision is more important. Vision is meant to be shared and readily comprehended so those exposed to it can act upon it.

John Welch was CEO of General Electric for twenty years, during which time he turned the slow-moving, struggling giant of a company into a dynamic, fast-growing business, increasing the value of the company from $13 billion to several hundred billion.[7] He took every public and corporate opportunity in executive meetings, public-speaking venues, publications, interviews, and private conversations to drive the vision home to people. It was not a one-time announcement or a plaque on the wall, but a continual exposure to the light of his vision for everyone and anyone he touched.

Managers were given free rein to run their business units as they saw best, but they had to conform to the vision of John Welch, which included adapting to change and striving to do better. He crafted a true vision-led organization instead of a leader-centered organization. As my friend Eric Beck, founder of Total Integration, often says, "Vision drives decision. A leader-centered organization needs access to the leader to make decisions while a vision-led organization only needs access to the vision to make decisions." Which do you think is more fruitful?

However it originates, the vision must be a shared vision. The purpose of the vision, after all, is to stimulate action and achieve results, not simply impress folks with lofty prose. If a vision is to shape the future and drive decision, then the leader and others in leadership roles must communicate it broadly, consistently, and continuously until it becomes an integral part of the corporate culture. At the foundation where I was helping a very talented team to build a $100 million endowment in eighteen months or less, this step was crucial. Joseph Johnson, the CEO, took a few days and developed a narrative or short story describing a day in the life of various personnel at some point in the future. It read like a novel and moved everyone like a high-impact adventure movie! Everyone wanted to be part of it! He has attracted the highest-quality people from world-class corporate backgrounds who want to be part of this exciting vision.

Joseph understands the power of vision and invests heavily and regularly in it. In fact, with some of the early funding, he produced a fourteen-minute video describing the vision of the business school he is funding. You can see it at www.SpireSchoolOfBusiness.com. Some folks thought it wasteful to invest in vision, but the video began paying dividends as soon as folks watched it. Furthermore, Joseph knows he must constantly position the leaves (team members) so they can be nourished by the vision, so he holds weekly meetings that are broadcast via Webcast across the country so everyone can attend. This investment in vision not only serves as a tool to fuel drive, effort, and commitment, but it also helps weed out folks who are there more for the paycheck than the vision.

Vision will die when it is out of sight, much as a plant will die without light. Always keep it part of the corporate dialogue.

Another example is my friend Wes Cantrell, who began his career with Lanier Corporation as a service tech servicing dictating machines after graduating from technical school in 1955. By the time he was twenty-seven, Wes was moved to Baton Rouge to assume the role of district manager. Recently Wes told me "the rest of the story" about how his meteoric climb up the corporate ladder came about. He recalled how his boss from Atlanta called him up to headquarters to share his vision of the future with him. Over dinner that fateful night, Wes heard for the first time what his boss wanted Lanier to become. It included buying out all their suppliers, including the copier supplier (which at the time was 3M), and that they would become a national, then an international company with offices all over the world. This was a big dream for what was then a small, regional company in the Southeast with annual revenues of about $5 million.

Wes got fired up by the vision. He went back to the office in Baton Rouge and passed on the vision in all its grandeur to the team members he was responsible for. He told them that someday he would fly over the city of Baton Rouge in a corporate jet and call them from the plane just to say hello! Wes told me that everything his boss told him in the vision literally came true, including the phone call from the corporate jet! The team in Baton Rouge was so fired up by the vision that, for Christmas, they gave Wes a map of the world with a plaque beneath that read, "This Is Your Territory." Everyone bought into the dream!

Wes took over as president of Lanier in 1977 when it was about a $93 million company and continued fueling the vision, acquiring 3M's copier/fax division, going international, becoming CEO in 1987, and eventually building the company into a $1.5 billion enterprise before retiring in 2001. He attributes much of his success to the power of vision and the importance of sharing that vision throughout the company and achieving buy-in from all stakeholders.

A vision features a compelling picture or image of what can become in the future. It builds enthusiasm and should provoke inspiration. It should stimulate people to care. It should "rally the troops to action." Your vision is a description of your "desired future state." Thus you'll create a vision statement describing your organization as you'd like it to be in, say, ten or more years. Note the emphasis on the future. The vision statement isn't true today. Rather, it describes the organization as you and your planning team would like it to become—in the future.

TEAM PARTICIPATION

People must see where they fit, what they contribute, and how their contribution can be measured; otherwise, they won't see themselves in it or make a significant contribution to the vision. It's not enough to tell them where the team is going. You need to make sure every team member can articulate their role in fulfilling the vision. They need to understand how their job, their function, their role directly contributes to the vision. When they buy into the vision and clearly understand their role, they will make a valuable contribution.

Vision must be strategic (long term) to help avoid making numerous tactical mistakes, costing time and money, and it must be big enough to inspire and motivate. It should also connect to and articulate deeper values and hopes for the future. A vision can be the glue that holds everyone together in a group, organization, or movement. If the vision is big and inspiring enough, a vision, just by being powerfully stated, can set in motion the energy needed for its own attainment.

As you prepare to define your vision, remember to make it clear, concrete, and compelling. It should be a powerful force in your life that inspires and guides. A life with vision is a life with focus. On page 107 I have prepared a worksheet that will help you outline the vision and focus for your life. If you really want to see your vision become a reality, and you need a little help, these seven steps are the key.

1. Find the vision.

Be clear. Be specific. Be compelling. Be descriptive. Write until it moves you. This doesn't need to be succinct. Describe in vivid detail the emotion, the impact on others, the scope, size, and timetable. This is not a picture of what is, but rather what you dream it to be. It may take ten or twenty years to get there. This is not a short-term thing but a long-term vision. Make it so clear and so real that you can see it in detail, feel the emotion, even smell and taste it.

2. Objectives

Identify specific goals with a timeline that must be accomplished to achieve the vision. This is critical. What are the markers along the way that you must hit to achieve the vision? Break the vision down into much smaller achievable goals. While setting annual goals is helpful, be sure to use thirty-, sixty-, or ninety-day goals as well.

3. Core beliefs

Establish right thinking. What you believe dramatically affects your result. I am not speaking about what you know, but rather about what you truly believe at a core level. For example, I have helped clients put millions of dollars in their corporate and private coffers and was happy to do so. But at a very deep, unconscious level, I discovered that I was uncomfortable ever having that kind of wealth. Intellectually I had no problem with it and could argue that case quite well, but at a gut level I was uncomfortable. I believed that somehow I shouldn't prosper that abundantly. I realized that I also had a cheap streak, which for me personally sprung from a lack mentality. Once exposed, I began changing my gut beliefs to align with what I knew to be true, and that opened things up for me.

Examine yourself. There are lies you believe and don't even realize you believe. One way to find out what you really believe is to observe what you do. After all, what you do represents more accurately what you really believe than anything else. Want to know what I believe? Watch what I do! The same is true for you. One day while pondering that by a hotel swimming pool, I asked God if I was cheap. After all, I would always take home all the bars of soap and shampoo bottles from each night's stay at the hotel. I hadn't paid for soap or shampoo for years! To my surprise, He answered, "Is the water wet?"

That was a real eye-opener for me and the beginning of a journey of self-discovery. I looked at all the ways I was cheap, and there were many! Then I began practicing abundance in each area, be that tipping generously at a restaurant, leaving shampoo at the hotel I didn't need, giving generously to others in need, and so on. As my hand relaxed its grip on material riches, our prosperity increased. It became evident to me that you can hold more in your hand when it is open than when it is clenched tightly.

Here's another important and simple way of testing what you really believe. List out the key beliefs you purport to hold, and then say them aloud in the first person. "I am increasing in wealth and health every day. I am increasingly generous every day. I love to give more than I receive. I am filled with abundance in every good thing." Make up your own list of positive confessions, but notice how you feel when you say them. If you only believe them intellectually but not at a heart level, you will feel uncomfortable saying them aloud and, even more so, saying them to someone else. You have no problem telling someone else your name or your profession or even that you are sick or experiencing lack, but try saying something positive about yourself, and the dynamic quickly changes.

Replace all the negative things you believe with truth. Write out the truth. Read it aloud. Tell someone else. Get comfortable with the truth. When I took on the role of endowment director with a foundation, I was initially uncomfortable sharing with folks our rather ambitious goal of growing the endowment from $10 million to $100 million of value in about eighteen months. It seemed like such a large number at the time. After we crossed the $50 million mark in about six months, that $100 million number no longer seemed big. Everyone got quite comfortable with it, and, in fact, the goal was then doubled!

4. Understanding

This is about what you know. I call it KIWI (knowledge, inspiration, wisdom, and ideas). Create a system for storing and accessing your knowledge, your inspirations, your wisdom, and your great ideas. Most of us have forgotten most of what we have read and most of the great ideas we had at one time or another. When you read a good book, consider writing a short book report. It will help you store up the key ideas in your memory, plus you can then store it in your hard drive or binder for easy future reference. Take the time to capture the key thoughts that spoke to you most, and put them in a separate, easy-to-find location.

Do the same with your inspirations and ideas. Collect them in a file folder, journal, or Word file, but collect them where you will easily access them. You may not be able to act on them now, but they may well be for an appointed time in the future. What wisdom have you gained? Write it down. Put it somewhere where you can refer back to it. If you forget what you learned, you may well have to learn those lessons all over again.

With respect to this exercise, write out the knowledge, wisdom, and ideas you have that will help you realize your vision. If you lack wisdom, seek it out from wise counselors who have already accomplished something similar. If you lack knowledge, go get it. Sign up for a class, a course, or a seminar. Buy books, CDs, or DVDs. Pick the brains of others who are doing what you want to do. Don't let ignorance be your enemy. Conquer it by pursuing knowledge and wisdom. The inspiration and ideas will flow out of that.

5. Strengths

I call this *playing your zone*. We all have to do things we are not good at. As much as possible, however, stick to your strengths. That's where you excel. When you are not in your zone, you are vulnerable. A rabbit is safe in the thicket. That's his zone. Put him in an open field, and he's easy prey for a hawk or other predator. Write out your most prominent strengths. Assign yourself activities that play to those strengths. When you are in your zone, you are playing at your best, your strength is renewed, and you love your work. It's what you were meant to do.

Don't leave weak areas unattended just because you don't like them, or you will get bit on the behind and won't like it at all! As much as possible, delegate your weak areas to others who are strong in them. Just because you delegate them doesn't mean you relieve yourself of responsibility. This is crucial. If you delegate the accounting, for example, to a trusted employee but never check the books to see if everything is in sync with your expectations and requirements, they may be interpreting your intentions differently than you had planned. Know the condition of your books, of your customers, and of your inventory. You don't have to do the physical count, but pay close attention to the state of affairs in everything you delegate. If you don't, your weakness that you delegated can still be your downfall!

Years ago when my wife and I had a publishing company, we were busy introducing new products and growing our company when our administrator took a temporary leave for double hip replacement surgery. Then tragedy hit, and my wife's son was killed in a car wreck. She withdrew from the business completely, and I threw myself into it more fully—both of us dealing with our grief in different ways. Sales soared by 85 percent, but so did our receivables. I had delegated that to others and was not monitoring our progress. We ended up with over a thousand stores who were overdue in paying us, and we almost went bust! We got focused and paid very close attention on a daily basis to the progress. We got things back on track and averted financial tragedy, eventually entertaining and accepting an offer from a bigger publisher to acquire our little company for a reasonable profit.

6. Everyday habits

Think of three things you're not doing consistently that if you did consistently would have a strong, positive impact on your life and help you realize your vision. Most successful people realize they have to take control of their actions, and they take the time to purposefully develop a few specific habits that will bring them closer to their life purpose. Once you've identified the habits you want to cultivate, find someone who can either join you in that habit or help hold you accountable.

Forming a good habit is like catching a current in the sea. It gives you acceleration and advantage. Most of us consider habits our enemy. They seem to enslave us to things we don't want to do. Breaking them requires huge effort. Instead of serving the demands of habits, make them serve you! The best way to do that is less about breaking old habits and more about establishing new habits in their place. When we do that, habits become our friends, our servants, and our allies!

Building good habits requires intentionality, while bad habits occur without intention. If you want habits to be your friend, you have to choose them. If you don't, you'll have bad ones by default. It's been said that "man becomes a slave to his constantly repeated acts: What he at first chooses, at last compels."[8] What we repeatedly do by choice ultimately becomes a compulsion, so we must make good choices, especially in the things we do often. As the twig bends, the tree inclines. That's the power of habits. Build good habits that will serve instead of enslave you all the days of your life.

We first make our habits, and then our habits make us. If you don't like what you've become or the direction you're headed, take a close look at your habits. Do an inventory of both your good habits and your bad ones. Bad habits require no effort at all to form, while good habits usually require exertion. But if you're willing to make the effort to impose good habits on yourself, they will in time become your friend and help you become all that your heart and dreams call for. It takes from twenty-one to thirty days to develop a new habit. If you'll invest the effort for a few short weeks, you can build into your life habits of excellence that will transform your life into one of excellence.

John Paul Getty said, "The individual who wants to reach the top in business must appreciate the might of the force of habit and must understand that practices are what create habits. He must be quick to break those habits that can break him and hasten to adopt those practices that will become the habits that help him achieve the success he desires."[9] One reason we fail at habits is that we sometimes bite off more than we can chew. If you haven't been exercising for years, and you decide that you're going to jog five miles a day because your neighbor does, you're probably in for a rude awakening!

The only reason bad habits persist is that they offer some satisfaction. You allow them to persist by not seeking any other better form of satisfying the same needs. Every habit, good or bad, is acquired and learned in the same way—finding it is a means of satisfaction. Ask yourself what need that bad habit is meeting, and then think of better ways you could meet that need.

Habits require discipline. Just the mention of that word conjures up images of pain and suffering that most of us want to avoid. In reality, discipline is simply being a disciple to an overriding purpose. Self-discipline comes from within, but how do you inspire such discipline? It is an important question, and applying the answer can significantly impact your future. James Allen once said, "You will become as small as your controlling desire and as great as your dominant aspiration."[10] Harry Truman added, "In reading the lives of great men, I found that the first victory they each won was over themselves...self-discipline with all of them came first."[11]

So, where do we find the intestinal fortitude to obtain self-discipline? Solomon said, "Where there is no revelation [vision], the people cast off restraint."[12] Visionless people have no discipline! Vision is the key to discipline. With a vision, the people use restraint. For example, an eight-year-old Olympic skater hopeful is in his parent's bedroom at 3:00 a.m. getting them up to take him to the skating rink for early practice. Whereas the child without vision is in the bed sleeping until his parents drag him out of bed and drive the sleepy youth to the practice rink. Is there an area where you lack discipline—perhaps with exercise, spiritual development, or family time? Perhaps you are not willing to do the grunt work on the job. Whatever it is, remember, vision precedes discipline.

7. Detailed plan

This maps out the path to achieving the objectives. It contains the specific steps needed to accomplish each objective. It answers the HOW question. It includes specifics on timing, staffing, support, methods, location, and so on. If it's not written down, it's not a plan. Write it down as if you were assigning the job of completing it to someone else and you were not going to be available for questions.

Until you take the time to put your goals in writing, along with a written plan on how to achieve those goals, you only have a wish, a fantasy, and a nice place to visit in your mind, but you will never get there in real life. Now, a plan is no guarantee for success. Not all who plan succeed, but all who succeed have a plan. Putting it in writing clarifies your thoughts and can expose the flaws in your thinking. If it is not worth taking the time to plan, either the goal is not worth achieving or you are not serious about reaching your goal. Make your plan a series of steps that, taken individually, are absurdly easy. Avoid broad statements like, "Become salesperson of the year and get promoted to regional manager." You need to identify what specific steps you are going to take on a daily basis that will allow you to become the salesperson of the year—how many calls a day, how many presentations, and what the average size of a sale will be. What is your presentation going to look like, and how are you going to get it to that point? Break the big goal into a series of little goals that are easily achievable.

USE THIS SECTION AS YOUR **VISION** WORKSHEET

F IND THE VISION:

_____

_____

O BJECTIVES:

_____

_____

C ORE BELIEFS:

_____

_____

U NDERSTANDING:

_____

_____

S TRENGTHS:

_____

_____

E VERYDAY HABITS:

_____

_____

D ETAILED PLAN:

_____

_____

I will build a motor car for the great multitude...it will be so low in price that no man making a good salary will be unable to own one and enjoy with his family the blessings of hours of pleasure in God's great open spaces....When I'm through, everybody will be able to afford one and everyone will have one...the automobile will be taken for granted and will give a large number of men employment at good wages.[13]

HENRY FORD

CONCLUDING THOUGHTS ON **VISION** ...

1. **No vision...no victory.** If you don't have a vision, complete with objectives, strategies, practices, and a plan, you're just dreaming.

2. **Know vision...know victory.** Once you know the vision, and everyone on the team knows it as well, and you have clear-cut objectives with strategies, practices, and a plan and everyone knows their role and how they will be measured, you are well on your way to victory!

3. **What stirs passion in you?** This is a clue to your purpose from which your vision will spring forth. Invest your life in a field that matters to you.

4. **Write the vision down.** This will take time, but it can pay big dividends. When interviewing someone you're interested in having join your company, have them read the vision and tell you where they think they fit into it and the contribution they believe they can contribute to it.

5 **Make it plain.** It should be that anyone reading the vision gets it! They shouldn't need further explanation. If they do, it's not yet clear.

6 **Every vision has an appointed time for its fulfillment.** Every good vision has a time when things come together to make it real. You will be tested. The vision will be tested. The team will be tested. Stay true to the vision. David Green, listed on the Forbes 400 wealthiest men, is founder of Hobby Lobby retail stores. Early in David's quest for his vision, the power company came to the store to shut the power off. After much pleading from David, the power company gave Hobby Lobby one more day to come up with the $3600 necessary to get caught up. They had enough sales that day to pay the electric bill, but the water got shut off a few days later.[14] The early days were a tremendous struggle, but every significant vision has significant trials. Will you persevere? Great vision is not for the faint of heart. In fact, I believe the skills necessary to steward the vision are forged in the crucible of fiery trials, especially in the start-up phase.

7 **Don't let a wound knock you off course.** We all take some incoming hits along the way. Many times we have no one to blame but ourselves, but don't wallow in it. Get back up. Keep going. Solomon said, "A good man falls seven times, but gets back up again."[15] I read a quote one time that speaks to me still: "Success consists of getting up one more time than you are knocked down."[16] Expect some rough patches, but don't give up because of them.

8 **An overnight success is not overnight.** If your vision is really compelling and exciting, you will spend a lot of hours in the furnace of affliction to see it through to fruition. There will be plenty of lonely hours when you fight the demons of doubt. If you faint in the hour of your trial, your strength is small, so press on. Weeping may endure for the night, but joy comes in the morning. When your breakthrough happens, people will think you were an overnight success, but you will know the truth and quietly smile.

ACTION STEPS

On a separate piece of paper, complete the following:

Seven questions you should ask when defining your corporate vision

1 *WHOM* do you serve internally and externally? Define your target market, not the fringe. You might serve more than one target or niche, and that's fine, but identify them. Drill down and be very specific. Get a clear picture of the profile of those you intend to serve.

2 *WHY* do you serve those interests? At the foundation I serve, there are economic goals and rewards for success, but the overriding reason people joined the organization was about the end result they believe the business school will serve. Generally speaking, people are motivated more by meaning than by money.

3 *WHERE* are the boundaries of your reach? Define the boundaries by whatever reference makes sense. This could be geographic, psychographic, demographic, or even philosophical. Knowing your boundaries keeps you out of unnecessary trouble. Sufficient for the day is the trouble in your own sphere of responsibility and calling.

4 *HOW* will you accomplish the vision? What are the specific actions that will be taken to apprehend the vision? Who is responsible for what part? Get clear on everyone's contribution, and make sure they are clear on it as well.

5 **WHEN** *will you know if you have succeeded?*
What measurable objectives must be realized
that allow you and the team members to know
they have accomplished the vision? Where is
the finish line? If you want "to be the best" in
the industry, what does that look like? What
measurables will establish you as being the
best? Is there some kind of certification? If you
are ambiguous about this, your team will be
too, and the vision becomes just another piece
of wall art.

6 **WHAT** *does that look like from all angles?* How
does your spouse see the vision? What about
the employees? Look at it from their perspective. What about your customers? What if they
read your vision; would they be energized by
it or feel like a target? How about vendors or
shareholders? Consider the impact of the vision
on everyone involved so that it energizes and
inspires them.

7 **WHAT** *is your contribution back to the world
around you?* As you achieve the vision, how will
you consciously contribute back? Have specific
goals for giving back along the way. Don't wait
until the vision is fully realized. Give back incrementally along the way. It will make the journey
far more rewarding.

■ ■ ■ ■

WEALTH SECRET #3

ENTER THE "NO PEST ZONE"
7 Natural Laws to Get Control of Your Time

> Until you value yourself, you will not value your time.
> Until you value your time, you will not do anything
> with it.[1]
>
> M. Scott Peck

> In truth, people can generally make time for what they
> choose to do; it is not really the time but the will that
> is lacking.[2]
>
> Sir John Lubbock

> The bad news is time flies. The good news is you're
> the pilot.[3]
>
> Michael Altshuler

O NLY TWO THINGS CAN TAKE OUT A TREE IN THE RAINFOREST," said our guide Dr. Helena Fortunato of the Smithsonian Institute. She volunteered this simple but, for me, life-changing fact as we walked along the path in the cool of the shade afforded us by the lush overhead canopy. "Other than lightning or being cut down by man, only two things can cripple or kill a tree," she said. "Pests and pathogens."

That set lights and bells off for me. I was already looking at trees as mini-corporations and the rainforest as being representative of the whole economy, so to hear that there were only two things to deal with was very compelling to me. I mean, who hasn't had to deal with pests? I was also pretty sure I understood what would constitute pathogens in a business setting. Just as with plants, those same two predators can diminish or end the quality of our life and business. It was imperative that I find out more about these two predators.

I headed back to the Gamboa Rainforest Resort on the Chagres River, where I was given access to their private library of hundreds of white papers written by Smithsonian scientists over the years who had studied this and a host of other phenomena. I also acquired books and other resources while at the research center. As it turned out, there was an incredible study done on Barro Colorado Island in the Panama Canal. Some researchers had taken thirty-five pairs of cuttings from native shrubs and planted them in an open area with lots of sunlight. They placed a fine mesh over the top of all of them, but for half of them, they completely enclosed the plant in fine mesh to keep out the pests.

They all got the same amount of light, water, and air, but 50 percent of them were protected from pests. Twenty months later, the fully protected shrubs were five and a half times bigger and growing at ten times the rate of the unprotected shrubs! Twenty-two percent of the protected plants flowered whereas no exposed plants flowered.[4] That's an incredible revelation for anyone in business! If you can find a way to keep the pests out of your life, not only can you experience much faster growth and greater market share than your competitors, but also your business will be self-replicating and sustainable. For the record, the plants covered with mesh still experienced the effects of pests, presumably through the soil. The consumption rate of the plants by pests was cut from 37 percent on exposed plants to 17 percent on protected plants, but that was enough to facilitate a growth differential by a factor of tenfold! What would happen if you could eradicate the last 17 percent?

PESTS AND PATHOGENS COMPARISON

Before we go any further, let's take a look at the difference between pests and pathogens and begin to identify them so we can deal with them.

 Both come from the outside.

 Pathogens eat us from the inside out.

Pests eat us from the outside in.

Pests consume what we produce.

Pathogens affect our ability to produce.

Pests affect our "doing well."

Pathogens affect our "well-being."

Pests include interruptions, distractions, diversions, things that divide our attention, and consume resources. Pests may include irrelevant vendors, preoccupation with sports, news headlines, e-mail, friends, or co-workers who consume your time and energy.

Pathogens include mind-sets, strongholds, behavior patterns, bad habits, automatic responses, and lies we believe that debilitate us. Pathogens may include poor self-image, overly important self-image, insecurity, fear, apathy, scarcity mentality, greed, and anger.

Pests engage us in a battle for what we choose and how we act. They compete for time and energy and eat away our profits.

Pathogens engage us in a battle for our mind—the *way* we think, the *way* we process information, the *way* we view the circumstances in which we find ourselves.

They compete for control of our mind, will, and emotions. They compete for our *soul*.

 We *see* the effect of pests.

 We *feel* the effect of pathogens.

 If we don't have a strategy, a plan, a way, and a habit of countering pests, we will be consumed. We will live, but we will produce nothing meaningful.

 If we don't have a way of curing our pathogens and defending against them, we accept sickness as the norm, we will grow (but not much), and, in the end, we will wither and not bloom.

 Pests come and go, come and go. They keep coming but are easily scared away.

Pathogens come less often, usually in the formative stages, but come to stay and are harder to rid yourself of.

THE HIGH PRICE OF PESTS

We are going to deal with pathogens in the next chapter, but for now I want to introduce you to some surprising facts. Did you know that the average worker is interrupted by an e-mail, phone call, or simple tap on the shoulder on average every eleven minutes? A study by *TIME* magazine has warned that such interruptions can lead to a host of psychological disorders in workers, as well as raising stress levels and reducing productivity.[5] Researchers studying a random sample of office workers found they got an average of just eleven minutes clear time to a project before being distracted by an e-mail, phone call, or verbal interruption from a manager or colleague. According to the magazine, it took an average of twenty-five minutes to return to a task after being disturbed! No wonder pests are so effective at limiting growth and productivity. Adding to that, psychiatrist Edward Hallowell told *TIME* magazine that he has seen a tenfold rise in the number of patients with work-induced attention deficit disorder. "They complained that they were more irritable than they wanted to be," he said. "Their productivity was declining. They couldn't get organized." Apparently adult attention deficit disorder took hold "when we get so overloaded with incoming messages and competing tasks that we are unable to prioritize," according to the article.[6]

The *TIME* article also found interruptions now took up an average of 2.1 hours of every working day, or 28 percent of the average person's nine-to-five schedule, including the time to recover your train of thought following an interruption. That's the equivalent of three months of work time![7] A study done by an insurance company shows that working from home, where there are often fewer interruptions, made workers more productive.[8] In terms of lost wages and reduced productivity, it is estimated that workplace interruptions cost the U.S. economy $588 billion a year.[9] The battle for your concentrated, uninterrupted work effort is subtle but intense. The effect of an interruption seems minor at the moment, but it is, in fact, substantial and cumulative.

Furthermore, as it turns out, estimates vary, but approximately 15 percent of the annual leaf production is consumed by pests. What's interesting is that damage rates to young leaves averages 20 times higher than damage rates to mature leaves. In fact, 70 percent of all damage over the typical 2.5-year life span of a leaf occurs during the brief few weeks of leaf expansion or about 4 percent of its life span.[10] Of course, a lot of the new leaves never survive being new. They don't get to mature.

It seems in business that the wise ones know how to focus. They know how to get things done. You can see them working, and you know not to bother them. There's an intensity about them that seems to carry a warning: "Disturb at your own risk!" The young ones (the newbies) are easily distracted and tend to be less productive, and many never mature to get to the next level in their career. They are stuck in a rut. They are constantly giving their time to pests, having never learned how to gain control of their time and their life. Similarly, when a new opportunity opens up, just like a new leaf emerging in the forest, it will attract new pests by the droves. Everyone wants in on the new thing. It takes experience, wisdom, and discipline to keep the pests away from the new opportunity.

We let the pests in oftentimes because we buy into the overrated idea of multitasking. We all multitask all the time. We breathe and walk and chew gum and observe the world around us while thinking about work, but when it comes to getting something accomplished, nothing is more powerful than monotasking. It's simply the power of focus. The more focused you are, the more intense you become and the more powerful your effort—plain and simple. Except for emergencies, a simple rule of thumb for getting things done is, "One thing at a time—the big thing—at the right time." Never allow the task you are working on to be infringed upon, nor let it take away from the next task its appropriate time of focus.

People with average skill but intense focus have accomplished results normally attributed to genius. It takes tremendous strength to achieve, and a lot of that strength is spent on resisting the things that clamor for your attention. The appeals are endless—Internet, e-mail, news, sports, telephone, fax, pager, beeper, text message, someone else's phone or beeper, voices, traffic, family, friends, vendors, and even customers. Every appeal for your attention requires energy just to ignore it and keep your mind focused on the business at hand. You have to bring every thought captive and into obedience to the task at hand. Overcoming distractions and focusing your mind is the biggest challenge of the day. The work itself is a pleasure and rewarding. The exhaustion comes from resisting the distractions and maintaining focus.

When I was a child spending summers at our cottage on Lake Simcoe in Ontario, I was a menace to ants. The means of my cruelty to ants was by harnessing the light of the sun with a magnifying glass into a very narrow, highly focused beam of light. The ants would be walking around their anthill enjoying the warm sun while I was trying carefully to focus that light into a powerful ray upon a moving ant. If successful, the beam of focused light would instantly fry the ant in a puff of smoke, and I would be off looking for my next victim. If I didn't focus enough, the ant was unharmed and the deed went undone.

In like fashion, our mind is capable of reacting to all manner of simultaneous input, but when it is focused upon a singular task, the resulting intensity and genius is powerful. To maximize this human potential, we need to keep pests at bay and master the discipline of focused attention. While it is exhausting, you can accomplish far more and of a higher quality than a diluted effort will get you.

The primary key to successfully focusing your mind on the tasks you wish to complete is harnessing what you give your attention to. While most of us have exercised our bodies at one time or another, few of us exercise our mind by training it to pay attention to certain things and ignore others. Just like Maslow's learning matrix, there are levels of attention we can attain with successive and increasing reward.

1. Involuntary attention

A gunshot, a backfire, a broken window, the sound of thunder, a swooping bird or plane, a fast-driving car, the ding of an incoming e-mail, the telephone ringer, a man in a suit at the beach, a cop in your rearview mirror, a flashing billboard, an upcoming holiday, birthday, or special event—all of these things, and many more, drop into our minds unexpectedly and capture our attention at least briefly. Sometimes they carry us away in a daydream for several minutes and tend to recur far more than we'd like. Involuntary attention requires no effort or intentionality on our part. It's automatic. It's reflex. It's annoying, and it's an expensive drain of our emotional and intellectual energy. Just as the plants fully protected with mesh still had pest damage, you too will never fully win the battle against these pests. You can, however, position yourself to be less exposed to them.

2. Conscious attention

This is the act of choosing to focus on a given task that you have prioritized for the present moment. It is an act of the will, despite the many other things vying for your attention. This is some of the most mentally exhaustive work you can do. While at first choosing to focus on the task can be strenuous, that is the price to pay if you're going to get to level three, which has the highest reward, the greatest joy, and the least stress.

3. Unconscious attention

This occurs when we have so disciplined our mind that it naturally focuses on the desired areas with relatively little effort. No amount of willpower will keep you focused on the same thing unless that thing is of interest and importance to you. Sometimes the fact is that you are not interested, but you must do the task. At times like that, appeal to a fundamental value or motive such as the benefit a loved one might receive or the reward you might enjoy upon completion. Sometimes you just think about the joy in front of you, and thus you endure the pain. The beauty of it is that what at first requires discipline to attend to now draws and allures you and rewards you for coming. What used to require much effort now comes with relative ease. The study of the rainforest is not a drain to me. It is of great interest and compels me. I study it for the lessons I can learn for my area of calling—the business arena. Now every tree, flower, bird, and bee is of interest to me. They are not distractions, but rather my passion. Eric Beck of Total Integration taught me the discipline of choosing to be fully present in the moment or task at hand. That one simple thought has helped me tremendously, and I force myself into the moment so I can get out of the moment what I am after. Soon it becomes a habit.

SEVEN NATURAL STRATEGIES FOR FIGHTING PESTS AND GETTING MORE DONE

The first step in becoming a good time manager is to observe the ways you currently spend your time. If you do it, write it down. Take notice of where your time goes and where and with whom you spend it. Take special note of the pests—those urgent, nagging, unimportant things that insist upon your attention now. Where do they come from? Where are you when they most frequently distract you? Who is the source? Once you are aware of where your time goes, it's much easier to make different choices.

Strategy #1

Leaf toughness

This is the most common and most effective strategy for leaves. When the leaves first appear, they are tender and cannot rely on toughness to defend them. They must remain tender until they reach their full size because they can't grow if the cell structure toughens up. During this brief time in their life span, they are most vulnerable. But once they reach their full size, they get tough and quite handily resist many pests. They spend most of their life span, however, in a toughened condition.

Get tough

To me, this speaks of getting tough with your pests. It's learning how to say no and not rewarding them for their untimely, unnecessary interruptions. Saying no for some people is a very hard thing to do, but it has tremendous rewards. Ask yourself, "Is this the wisest and best use of my time right now?" If you cannot respond positively to that question, say no to the opportunity.

What can you eliminate?

How does a pest know when a new leaf has toughened up? It doesn't make any headway when it attempts to consume the leaf. The leaf is unreceptive to the uninvited guest. Once your staff or your co-workers realize you are serious about your work, that you're unreceptive to their casual interruptions, they will leave you alone. If they get politely but firmly rebuffed when you are busy, they will quickly learn to leave you alone when you're working. Get serious. Don't reward interruption.

Track your every action for at least one day. Include everything, and then tally it up at the end of the day. How much of your day did you spend reading and/or answering unimportant e-mails? What about checking the news or stock market? How about phone calls? Look at not only the quirky, irregular things you do in a day but also the routines you have that have little or no payoff. What would happen if you simply didn't do them? What would happen if your computer crashed and you lost all those unanswered e-mails?

Try looking at it this way: Suppose you were leaving the country to travel thirty-nine hundred miles up the Amazon River to the headwaters coming high up out of the Peruvian Andes as a thin sheet of crystal clear water flowing down the side of a rock wall. It's the trip of a lifetime, and it's going to take you six weeks. Think of all the things that you won't do while you're gone, most of which will not be waiting for you upon your return. Those are the first things you can begin to eliminate now before you go to the Amazon, so that at least while you're home, you can either enjoy more free time or get more of the truly important things done.

Do you have a lot of clutter in your home or office? If so, chances are you have a lot of clutter in your schedule. First thing to do is remove the physical clutter from your life. Make a trip to The Salvation Army or local Goodwill center. What you can't give away, haul away. The way you do anything is typically the way you do everything. When your physical world is not cluttered, it is easier to order the rest of your life.

What can you automate?

In a conversation with a busy CEO client of mine, I explained the seven primary defense strategies of plant life in the rainforest. One of the first things he did was to change his message on his phone to ask all callers if they wouldn't mind sending him an e-mail instead of leaving a voice mail to increase the likelihood that he could respond in a timely manner. The number of people who opted not to leave him a message was significant, and many of those didn't bother with an e-mail either. His automated response to their demand on his time cost him no time whatsoever and reduced the amount of "time debt" he felt he had.

Dan Kennedy, one of the better known marketers of our time, is a man people seem to either love or hate, but no one can argue with his success in marketing. If you want to reach him though, you have to send him a fax! You can call his office, but he won't call you back. If you want to speak with him, you must make an appointment, and every minute is on the clock, so don't waste time talking about the weather! Making people send you a fax instead of using e-mail seems archaic, but it is a deliberate way of minimizing the pests. Because sending a message by fax instead of e-mail is a pain in the rear, only the very seriously interested customers or clients will bother. While you may think this counterproductive and limiting in nature, try getting a time slot with the man! Furthermore, he doesn't use a cell phone because he knows it will take away what little free time he does have. He says when he speaks at conferences he notices on the breaks everyone running outside and getting on their cell phone to return calls or make new ones, while he peacefully sits down in a comfy sofa chair and actually takes a break.

The bottom line here is to see what system you can put in place to handle routine things like incoming communication, outgoing responses, and customer service. Consider using auto-responders with your e-mail that lower the expectation for a response except for the things you consider high priority. We get more inquiries in a day from wonderful people the world over who are responding to our Web site, our coaching e-mails, or perhaps our online store than I can even consider responding to, even though I wish I could respond to all of them. We have had to identify the broad categories of inquiries and develop auto-responders for each one just to keep our inside staff at the most productive levels.

Strategy #2

Secondary metabolites

This is an automatic chemical defense, making the plant undesirable, even deadly if eaten. Think chemical warfare. This is most common in young leaves that are tender and need to remain tender while growing, yet be protected. Insects may get a bite or two, but they are quickly turned away by the chemical defense. This investment in chemical defense is expensive for the plant but only has to continue until the leaf is fully grown, at which time most species will toughen up and be impenetrable to the majority of pests, and the chemical compounds are redeployed for other less toxic uses.

Get serious

You are never more vulnerable than when you are starting a new enterprise, working on a new project, or beginning a new job. Breaking the inertia, finding your groove, and getting into the zone are examples of what must happen to make any real progress. Pests seem to thrive, even congregate, around the new thing or idea where all the excitement, the attention, and the resources are focused. They come under the guise of wanting to help or some other innocent excuse, but the end result is the same—they deplete you of your energy, rob you of your time, and drastically reduce your productivity. As a result, you may not ever break through the inertia, overcome the obstacles, or meet the challenge of the new endeavor.

This is a very serious concern, yet most people fail to recognize its deadly consequence. Dreams are bled dry, hopes are deferred, and success is stalled if not altogether eliminated. And it happens in slow motion with smiles all around. The pests come as friends and may even be your friends, but their good intentions should not be allowed to pull you off the mission. They remind me of the strangler fig. It starts out as a seed in a bird dropping on the branch of a tree. It begins its life as an epiphyte (air plant) and grows harmlessly on the branch. It even looks nice. But then it sends down aerial roots to the ground where it takes hold and begins to build its own support system. That still seems harmless enough, but it then sends up branches to hog the sunlight and rob the original tree of its power and its energy, its vision if you will. Slowly but surely, it encases the host tree, suffocating it gently and almost without notice. If it had been done over a period of thirty minutes instead of thirty years, it would have been horrific to watch.

That's the way so many pests operate. They just need your help on this. They just have a question about that. It all seems legitimate, but if you don't get a handle on it and control their access to you, the thing you are working on will never see the light of day! This is never more urgent than when starting something new. If you don't rigorously defend your time when starting something new, it will not do well with neglect and will die a slow death or live out a deficient life.

You must get brutal with the pests who would rob you of the thing you are called and wired to do with your life. I am not suggesting you use chemical weapons or create physical harm, of course. I am suggesting that you take it all very seriously. Explain to your co-workers, your employees, your friends, and your family that when you are working on that project, you don't want any interruptions unless the building is burning down and they need help getting everyone out! If you have a vendor who pesters you, remove him from your vendor list. Create a consequence that shows you mean business. It's that important, and the fight over your time and attention will never be greater or more concentrated than when you are working on something new and important. Be prepared to fight the good fight!

Strategy #3

Delayed greening

Pest defense of any kind has a cost associated with it. Chemical defense is expensive, so some plants choose to delay the release of chlorophyll (the greening agent), which is the very thing pests are looking to consume, until the leaf can defend itself. Instead of being green, the leaves are pink, red, or even white and remain that color until the leaf has reached full size, toughened, and is better protected from pests. The lack of investment in chlorophyll is obvious to pests, and they waste little time and do little harm to plants with little resources to consume. Furthermore, the reddish coloration infers danger to would-be leaf-eating insects. Although there is, in fact, no danger involved, it is an additional way of warding off pests. It's rather like putting a sign on your house that says, "This home protected by Brinks Security," when, in fact, it isn't. It may give some burglars pause to reconsider their ill intentions on your home.

For some plants, the potential loss of leaf surface by having no protection is less expensive than what they would experience by investing in protective chemical agents. The cost of that option is further increased because having no green in the leaves also means reduced ability to turn sunlight into food.

Get strategic

Pests consume more than your time. They consume your money, your personnel, and your mental energy. Pests are always looking for target-rich environments where every target is rich in resources. In other words, it seems that the more you invest in someone, the greater the attack on their time, talent, and treasure. Therefore, it behooves you to qualify them in some way before investing a lot of resources.

Suppose you have people in your employ in positions that typically have a high turnover rate. You might want to make sure the new hire has the discipline, skill, character, and calling to be in that role for the long haul before you invest a lot of resources into them. For example, instead of paying for their college tuition, you may want to provide basic training at your office to equip them. If they mature, toughen up, and survive the first ninety days, you may want to provide a higher level of training at corporate head office or at the seminar downtown, or perhaps have them attend the annual conference to take them to the next level. If they don't survive the initial entry period with limited resources, you haven't lost much. If they do survive, they have demonstrated they can be trusted with greater resources.

What can you procrastinate?

Delay is not always a bad thing, especially if it's purposeful. I found quite accidentally that a few hundred e-mails I delayed responding to found another solution elsewhere. Just because someone has an emergency on his or her end doesn't necessarily constitute one on my end. A delayed response is a response, but it requires virtually no effort. Not everything deserves equal attention or immediate response. For example, while I am writing this book, I am only responding to e-mail from Jill Johnson, who is doing a wonderful job of being my research assistant. Her e-mails contain valuable information relevant to the task at hand. In order to receive her e-mail updates, I also receive a hundred other e-mails too, but I am delaying my response to them. Many of them won't matter in a few days, and most won't matter in a few weeks. The truly important ones will still be important at a time convenient to me.

Procrastination seems to only have a bad rap, but if used strategically, it can be a great time-management tool. Paying your bills once a month is a form of procrastination. Meeting with someone next week, when your schedule is better suited for it, is a form of procrastination or delay. Use delay for your advantage. The best public speakers use delay (a pause)...in the middle of a sentence, for example, to focus attention to a single moment, usually the next word or phrase. Delay is usually a better choice than a rash decision. If someone presents a new opportunity to you that requires investment, and they tell you that you have to decide now or miss it altogether, it is usually best to delay.

Don't get me wrong. Delay is not my modus operandi. I like action. I want a decision now! I want to put all the money on horse number nine! But I have found that delay, more times than not, if it is purposeful and has an end point in view, is best—not endless delay or mindless delay or senseless delay, but delay until a certain benchmark has been reached. That is strategic. Know your benchmarks. Know when to hold the investment of time, talent, or treasure, and know when to release it all and flood it with the necessary resources to take it to the next level. Evaluate the things you have rushed into that have cost you dearly, and weigh that against the times, if any, that making a rush judgment and investment has paid off, and you will likely see that purposeful procrastination pays!

Another example of using the delayed greening model for getting strategic is where you delay the input of valuable resources into a project, a product, or a new business unit until you can properly commit to it. Don't invest heavily early on. Start small. Test your assumptions. A lot of time and a lot of money are wasted by launching prematurely. Money is just time in folded form. When you waste money, you've wasted time. Test your ideas before investing big. The feedback will save you time and money. Every direct marketer knows to test his or her mail-out piece to small groups before investing big in the nationwide direct mail campaign.

Control events instead of falling prey to them. If they come calling before you are best equipped to respond, and where responding is going to get you off track and cost you time or treasure, delay your response to them. He who chooses the time of the battle has the advantage. When we choose the time to engage the activity, we reduce the amount of time it takes, improve the quality of the results we get, and, in the process, have far less stress. Get strategic and learn to use purposeful procrastination as a time-management tool.

Strategy #4
Altering leaf phenology

Another strategy used by plants to avoid being consumed by pests is to alter the timing of their leaf production (phenology). One strategy is to shift leaf production to peak during the season when most of their pests are rare, which is the dry season in most forests. Dry season in the rainforest, if it is long and dry enough, has a similar effect to the effect a cold harsh winter has on insects in cooler climate areas. The second strategy is to maximize their leaf production synchronously with other trees to create such a vast number of fresh, tender leaves in the forest so that the risk of loss is spread around more diversely. It's kind of like swimming across a small river in Africa with a few crocodiles on the bank. If you are the only one swimming across, you have a greater chance of only making it halfway, but if there is a stampede of wildebeests, all trying to get across the river, it is a sure thing a few of them won't make it but you have a better chance of being one that does.

Get synced

This is about synchronizing your busy work in such a way as to minimize the number of likely pests or maximizing the number of likely targets so you're less likely to be a target. Here's how it works:

Work when pests are rare

Have you ever worked on a holiday? Did you notice how much more you got done? No one called you or e-mailed you, and if they did, they weren't expecting a response. You probably got more done on that holiday than on the entire week before that day! I am not saying you should work holidays, but if you did, you could probably take two or three regular workdays off and still be ahead of the game. Another way is to come in early before everyone arrives or stay late. At my office, Cheryl usually comes in late so she can work in the evening hours where she has zero interruptions. Her productivity soars as is evidenced by the number of e-mails from her containing solutions to the day's challenges.

Some folks rise early and get their clarity for the day before everyone else cries for their attention. Others find their best uninterrupted time to be at night after the kids are in bed. I turn the ringer off of my personal extension, put the cell phone on mute, close my e-mail program and Internet Explorer, and close my office door after having given notice that unless the hurricane is a category four or more, I don't want to hear about it.

It doesn't have to be limited to a time when pests are rare; it can be a *place where pests are rare*. Next week (after finishing this book), my wife and I will be back in Central America, this time exploring the Costa Rican rainforest. I will not have my cell phone or laptop in the jungle, nor do I feel obligated to be plugged into client work while on assignment in the rainforest. We anticipate having plenty of quiet time at the resort situated on a thirty-acre coffee plantation to read, relax, and write. We will truly be insulated from all the business pests that we encounter at home and will get more out of our time together than we might otherwise experience.

This is a strategy I have used with clients over the years. For example, clients of mine will on occasion fly to where I live in Southwest Florida to get away from all the distractions of the office. We set up a "No Pest Zone" and meet for two or three days in highly focused, highly productive meetings by the pool, near the river, or whatever environment we choose. I lock myself in with them, and for that forty-eight- to seventy-two-hour period, we make more progress on key, strategic issues than we would accomplish in a month of meetings at their corporate office, plus they leave refreshed and recharged! As a result, they have made "No Pest Zones" a part of their operating strategy and routinely build it into their time-management philosophy.

Work when everyone is busy

When I first discovered the "No Pest Zone" concept, we had come back from the Panamanian rainforest, and I was laden down with research material from the Smithsonian. I sat out by the pool on our lanai, left my cell phone inside, my e-mail shut off, and immersed myself in the study of the rainforest. The science behind it is all a bit overwhelming with chemical formulas, graphs, charts, and a lot of words I had to look up in the dictionary online, but I was on a mission and would not be deterred. After a couple of days of intense study and note taking, I checked in with the office. Cheryl, my faithful administrator, wondered where I had been since getting home and was surprised by my silence and absence. I excitedly explained that I had set up a "No Pest Zone" and was getting more done than ever, to which she commented, "Well, while you were in your 'No Pest Zone,' I was not getting the usual number of calls and e-mails from you, and so I was able to get a whole lot more done too!"

It had never occurred to me that for Cheryl, I was the pest interrupting her productivity. I learned a valuable lesson that day: when you set up a "No Pest Zone" for yourself, you create the conditions for others to enjoy a similar benefit. The more people in the office working in a "No Pest

Zone," the less everyone else is distracted and the more the entire team gets done. When I shared my findings with my wife, Brenda, she told me she's been trying for years to get me to quit checking e-mail and answering everyone's calls when I was working on a project, and I wouldn't listen. She found it amusing that I had to go to the rainforest to learn what she has known and been telling me all along!

So here's how this works. Time your busy work when others are busy. If everyone else is preoccupied with a project or deadline, it creates a "No Pest Zone" opportunity for you. Synchronize your work for high productivity times when everyone is pressing toward the goal. Not only does it create fewer distractions for you, but equally important, it also builds a team momentum that has a synergistic effect. It's been shown that if two horses can each pull a dead weight of five thousand pounds, the two of them working at the same time, on the same thing, and pulling in the same direction can actually pull fifteen thousand pounds instead of the ten thousand you might have thought. The same is true at work. It's great if you are getting a lot done, but when the whole team is in sync and all working on a project, the whole is greater than the sum of the parts.

Another form of synchronization is when you synchronize related projects. Last year we were looking for a guest for our monthly teleseminar, and we were also looking for a new product to release to our subscribers. After reading John Muratori's excellent book *Rich Church Poor Church*, we invited him for an all-day teleseminar, which we recorded, transcribed, duplicated, and sold, all in one synchronous effort. We ended up with a CD series, an e-book, and a successful event all in one day. What activities or projects can you batch?

You can also batch physical objects, paperwork, and books. Experts say we lose an average of one hour a day looking for things. If you want more time, spend less time looking for what you need. Batch items or group them together so you know where to find them. Documentation is one thing, but document retrieval is another. Establish a place for everything, and then put everything in its place. I keep all my books on sales and marketing on one shelf, business strategy on another, and so on. One last tip for synchronizing: sync your "to do" list to your appointment calendar. By that I mean, make an appointment with yourself to complete your priority tasks. If you don't tie it down to a specific time to get done, it is much more likely to be left undone. Appointments are specific, and we tend to keep them much better than we fulfill our "to do" lists.

Strategy #5

Rapid leaf expansion

On Barro Colorado Island, I was shown a plant with leaves two feet long. That by itself was not too special, but then I was told that the day before, the leaves were only one foot long, and the day before that only six inches long, and the day before that only three inches long. Apparently they grow from bud to twenty-four inches in a week! The leaves do not invest in chemical defense and they don't get tough. Their strategy is simply to grow faster than they can be eaten!

Get motivated

I know a little about this topic. Peter Lowe heads up Get Motivated, the largest business seminar organization in the world with a veritable who's who of guest speakers. I've had the opportunity to speak at a number of his events and have seen and heard firsthand incredible stories of motivation and accomplishment. When I saw this plant in the rainforest with its large leaves and rapid growth strategy to outrun the pests, so to speak, I understood immediately what that was in business vernacular.

It's all about rapid bursts of concentrated energy, highly focused on a narrow task. For me, that's about setting aside short blocks of focused time for nothing but the project at hand. It's "making hay while the sun shines," because you never know what tomorrow holds. Find what motivates you and use it. A friend of mine in Canada was moving into a new home, and the grass for the yard had not yet been planted. There was a slight rise of about three feet from the side of the road passing by his house and the general elevation of the front yard and house. It had been raining recently, and he was trying to drive a five-ton truck full of furniture up the three-foot incline and over to the house for easy unloading.

He could get the front wheels over the incline but couldn't pull the back wheels up the slight hill. He had been trying for quite some time when I came along and had put wooden planks in the mud where the tires had gotten stuck, but still he couldn't get the loaded truck up the hill. At first, I offered to get behind the truck and push when he hit the gas. I've been less brilliant in my life, but that one stands out as quite memorable as I had mud and water spinning onto my face and clothes, and, of course, my extra body weight against the truck did not make the difference!

Wanting to help him and realizing it wasn't my physical strength he needed, I utilized the Get Motivated strategy. It's not sustainable, but it doesn't have to be. It just needs to work! I told him how he could get that truck over the hump and up the hill in less than sixty seconds if he would do exactly as I said—no questions asked! He agreed, so I asked him to imagine the communists were coming down the street (Reagan was president at the time), and when they got to the truck they were going to do unspeakable horrors to his wife and children unless he got in that truck right now and drove it up the hill and out of harm's way! I said it with a powerful sense of urgency and told him to GO!

Well, he jumped in the truck, backed it up further than ever, put it in drive, and hit the gas, almost tipping the truck over as it rocked its way up the hill, but up the hill it went and over—all in less than ten seconds. He simply provided himself with an artificial form of motivation, acted as though it were true, and solved a problem he had been working on for at least an hour. When I find myself with a short window of time before having to leave for an appointment or head off to the airport, I will often find a small project I can focus intently on with the hope of completing before I leave. It's amazing how much you can get done in a short time when you are highly motivated and completely focused.

The Pareto principle seems to bear this point out as well. It's where 80 percent of the effect comes from 20 percent of the effort. Good-sized companies with a well-established customer base will typically find that they get 80 percent of their revenue from 20 percent of their customers. Pareto found that 80 percent of the peas came from 20 percent of the pea pods in his garden. He also noticed that 80 percent of the wealth in his town was controlled by about 20 percent of the people. It's not a law, but things tend to work out relatively close to that ratio. So apply it to your work effort. Give a short burst of effort consuming 20 percent of your time, and watch how you will complete 80 percent of a normal day's work. The pests aren't used to that and have a hard time keeping up with you!

Strategy #6

Camouflage defense

Passionflower vines are an example of a plant that protects itself from pesky leaf-eating caterpillars. On occasion they will mimic leaf patterns of nearby trees to hide from butterflies. If a butterfly lays its eggs on one of the stems of the plant, the plant will shed that stem in order to dispose of the eggs. Passionflower vines also form yellow dots on their stems to make butterflies think that spot has already been taken. Camouflage is widely used in the rainforest when the plant or insect doesn't want to be noticed.

Get wisdom

There's an adage that says, "Be wise as a serpent and harmless as a dove." Have you ever wondered in what way a serpent is wise? Well, it turns out the wisdom spoken of is called *sagacious* wisdom. It means to have or show acute mental discernment and keen practical sense. Serpents are deemed wise because they are well aware of their environment, and even though they have fangs and are sometimes poisonous, they avoid confrontation with an enemy if at all possible. They are not looking for trouble and prefer to disappear in the tall grass.

The more you attract attention to yourself, the more pests will gather around you and feed upon your time, your wit, and your kindness until you have nothing left. They will move on or go home, but your workload remains, so be wise; don't compromise. When you have to get things done, make yourself invisible. Close your door. Don't answer your phone if you can get by with that. Save the social hour for breaks and after hours.

Strategy #7

Ant defense

The cecropia tree protects itself from pests by allowing armies of ants to feed on its sweet, liquid droplets. When we visited the Costa Rican rainforest, we saw firsthand how very protective the ants were of their bountiful food source and how, if you knock on the trunk, they will come running out of the partially hollowed tree trunk to attack you. The tree provides a natural and safe haven for the ants to dwell in, and the ants will fight to the death to protect the tree from anything that tries to attack it. Other plants offer nectar in exchange for defense from leaf-eating pests like caterpillars and ladybugs.

Get help

This one is easy. Get someone to run defense for you, screen your calls, handle the mail, and even answer e-mails for you if possible. As said earlier, if possible, create an automated response mechanism that minimizes the amount of direct time required from you. There is a tendency with entrepreneurs to do everything themselves, especially if they want to have it done right! If you are an entrepreneur who does that, your staff will probably let you keep on doing their job for them as long as you are willing to do it.

Maybe you can't hire a full-time assistant, but there are a lot of other possibilities from part-time help to virtual assistants, depending on the kind of help you need. If it can be done remotely over the Internet, you can employ an assistant for a few hours a day or week who will work on your project of research or data entry overseas when you are in bed sleeping.

The best combination is to minimize distractions, get organized, and work systematically through the priorities of the day's work. Set aside the appropriate amount of time for the task at hand, and then get it done. Push everything else aside while you complete the task; then you can focus on the next one. Don't let the worry of the next one impose on the current work at hand. Be sure to give yourself a mental and physical break when needed, as focus becomes increasingly difficult when you start getting brain fog or fatigued. I often stop my work and go for a walk with my wife around the block or over to the lake. It gets the blood flowing, the mind refreshed, and the oxygen circulating through my body. To succeed long term, maintain your health, get plenty of sleep, and eat healthy food.

ACTION STEPS

1 Identify your top three "pests" and which strategy you will take to eliminate or minimize their effect.

2 Set aside a "No Pest Zone" for one full day to focus on an important project.

■   ■   ■   ■

THE PATHOGEN PROBLEM
Defeating What's Been Eating You

Within you right now is the power to do things you never
dreamed possible. This power becomes available to you
just as soon as you can change your beliefs.[1]

MAXWELL MALTZ

Self-image sets the boundaries of individual
accomplishment.[2]

MAXWELL MALTZ

Attitude is a deep-seated, chosen belief, either positive
or negative that sets in motion corresponding behavior,
generally resulting in a self-fulfilling prophecy.

MICHAEL Q. PINK

PESTS CONSUME US FROM THE OUTSIDE IN, BUT PATHOGENS ARE
the unseen things that eat us from the inside out. The big question
in this chapter is, "What's eating you?" Ignoring disease, whether
physical or mental, does not make it go away. It allows it to grow unim-
peded. Not all disease is deadly, but all disease robs you of vitality and
life. In business that means lost profits, maybe a lost business, and even
lost dreams. Pathogens are those inner demons we struggle with that war
against our soul and cut into our quality of life, our sense of well-being,
and our desire to achieve. They consist of the lies we believe, the things
we fear, the pain we carry, and the image we see.

The attitude we carry in life is largely shaped by these four things, but the best news you will ever hear on this subject is also the most difficult—your attitude is always a choice! Once you accept responsibility for your attitude, life gets a whole lot better. You have little control over what comes at you in life, but you have full control of how you respond to it. Responding in a positive way improves not only the quality of the moment but also the actual outcomes you eventually experience. Let's take a look at the four attitude shapers that try to override your will.

THE LIES WE BELIEVE

All of us believe lies. If we knew which of the things we believed that were, in fact, false, we would stop believing them—or so you would hope. There are lies about ourselves, our worth, our potential, our problems, and our past that we believe but are not true. What's so insidious about the lies, besides the fact that we can't see them, is that they are deeply embedded in our heart. At an intellectual level we may well disavow those lies and say we don't believe them and be sincere, but if you want to know what you really believe, pay attention to what you do. It's the action that tells the story. Sometimes the lie is so deeply embedded that it has become part of us and we don't realize it.

Lies we believe hold us back in much the same way elephants are held back in the circus. When baby elephants are brought into the circus, a small rope is tied around their leg at one end and fastened to a stake or pole at the other to keep them from running away. As the elephants grow up, however, eventually weighing several tons, they can easily pull away from the stake and go free. The thing is, though, they don't. They grew up believing the rope defined their freedom or lack thereof, and as adult elephants, as soon as they feel the tug of the rope, they give in. They accept the limits of the rope even though they no longer apply. What they believe about the rope and its strength to hold them back is a lie.

We act on what we deeply believe. If that is a lie, we will produce bad fruit or no fruit at all. That's the way pathogens affect plants. They rob them of fruitfulness, eventually causing them to wither and die. Ask those closest to you to speak truth to you, to help you expose the lies you believe, and to affirm the truth they see in you. Don't be defensive.

Ask them for what they see to be your strengths and your weakness. Ask them what they think holds you back. Make it safe for them to tell you the truth, and they will. The truth may be uncomfortable at first, but it will set you free and lead you to fruitfulness.

THE THINGS WE FEAR

A lot of the things we fear are based in lies, but many are not. Fear is debilitating because it carries torment. Fear of job loss. Fear of revenue decline. Fear of lack. Fear of success. Fear of intimacy. Fear of man. Fear of failure. The list is endless. Only two things will dispel fear. The first is knowledge. The second is love. Fear flourishes in the darkness of ignorance. There was a time in the Middle Ages when the aristocrats stopped eating tomatoes because they believed tomatoes were poisonous. The peasants didn't get the memo and kept eating them without harmful effect. It turned out that the reason aristocrats were getting sick and even dying from eating tomatoes was because they were eating off of pewter plates and the acid in the tomatoes was leaching out the lead, causing lead poisoning.

The way to handle any fear is to first of all face it. As long as you're afraid to face your fears, they have control over you. Their power begins to break when you stop running or stop ignoring them and stare them down. In 1994 we took a big hit financially from our Guatemala venture. The bills had mounted up, and we were behind in everything. For a while I just piled up the bills because I didn't have the means to pay them and because, quite frankly, the fear in the pit of my stomach would rise up every time I thought about them. It all changed one day when I opened every bill, laid them on the floor around me in a circle, and faced them. I asked God for strength and wisdom, then began contacting the ones I owed and doing what I could. It wasn't long before the financial flow was back and the debts retired. The first thing that had to go was the fear.

Fear weakens you, sickens you, and defeats you. Treat it like the enemy it is. When you face it down, it will leave. Sometimes all you need is knowledge or information to quench the raging fire of fear. Sometimes it takes more. Just knowing you don't have to face the fear alone is a big help. There was a time back in the early eighties, after losing my firstborn child, my marriage, my business, and every dime I had, that I just didn't want to carry on. I was walking across a mostly frozen lake in Ontario one March night, partially hoping the ice would give way and end my misery. I was telling God how bad things were, and I could see in the night sky, as it were, my problems like a mountain looming overhead, each of them with a personality wanting to grant my wish and push me through the ice.

Something was holding them back, and, in that moment, a fresh resolve came to my soul. The story of David and Goliath came to mind, and somehow I knew I didn't have to face this trial alone. There was another way out. I announced to the night sky that I would not succumb to the depression but would, like David, find a way to defeat that mountain of losses in my life. The next morning walking from the chalet to the lodge where I was attending company sales training, I saw a nearby mountain covered in snow that I had tried unsuccessfully to ski downhill on the day before, using cross-country skis. Still in the zone from the night before, I spoke to the mountain and said, "I'm coming back here tonight, and I'm going to ski down you until I can ski down you blindfolded."

The fact that I was not a skier and had the wrong kind of skis for downhill skiing notwithstanding, I returned that evening with a friend, strapped on some skis, and on my first attempt made it top to bottom without falling. True to my vow, I climbed back up to the top, borrowed my friend's black scarf, blindfolded myself, and asked him for a shove to get me started downhill. I must confess, there's nothing quite like the rush of skiing downhill on cross-country skis when you are not a skier and your eyes are tightly shut with a blindfold! The wind is rushing past your face, your imagination is running wild, and your adrenalin is pumping through your veins like water through a fire hose in a three-alarm fire! Amazingly, I made it top to bottom without falling. The first thing I heard in my head when I came to a stop was that it was just luck that I made it without falling.

This was not about being macho or being a show-off. This was for me a spiritual battle. I couldn't leave my fate to luck. I had to know I could really beat that mountain blindfolded. I hiked back up to the top, blindfolded myself a second time, and skied top to bottom without falling. I believe the same force that guided David's stone into Goliath's skull was the same force that kept me safe on my way down the hill. Upon opening my eyes not too far from a tree at the bottom of the slope, I looked up at the mountain and exclaimed, "I beat you!" For me, beating that physical mountain was the first step in facing my fears, accepting God's help, and beginning my path back to healing and happiness. When it comes to fear, don't give it any quarter!

THE PAIN WE CARRY

This is the pain we have buried deep within us. We don't choose it. We don't want it, and we may not know we have it. But it's there, and it surfaces when we least expect it. Many of us carry unresolved pain from abuse, abandonment, or loss that we have no idea how to relieve. A frequent cause of depression, it may also lead to addictions of various kinds and have substantial impact on work performance. In fact, more workers are absent from work because of stress and anxiety than due to physical illness or injury. According to a recent large-scale study published by the Rand Corporation, "Depression results in more days in bed than many other ailments (such as ulcers, diabetes, high blood pressure and arthritis)."[3] The *American Journal of Psychiatry* says, "Those with symptoms of depression are seven times more likely to experience lowered productivity on the job than those without such symptoms."[4]

According to the Surgeon General, one in five adults (20 percent) will experience a diagnosable mental illness in any given year. At any one time, one employee in twenty is experiencing depression. About 15 percent of those will also experience "substance abuse." Among those of working age, it is estimated that the prevalence of mental illness and/or substance abuse in any given year approaches 25 percent with the cost to employers annually being estimated at $80 to $100 billion.[5] Ronald Kessler, a professor of health-care policy at Harvard Medical School, added that "depression is particularly likely to have ripple effects on other employees. One employee who is depressed can affect 20 coworkers."[6]

Not only is there an economic cost, but depression also affects productivity, judgment, the mind-set of the team, and total job performance. Just the inability to concentrate fully, process information, and make decisions can lead to costly errors and even injury. Add to this the fact that workers suffering with depression have high rates of absenteeism and other off-the-job problems, and it all gets very costly. According to Keith Dixon, PhD, president of Cigna Behavioral Health, "Depression results in 400 million lost work days a year and is a huge drag on industrial productivity. Companies in our economy now need to compete globally, and the direct and indirect costs of depression are serious threats to our economic security in a vastly altered competitive landscape."[7]

There is another pain we sometimes have. It's the pain we choose to hold on to. But holding on to the pain and the anger only serves to keep us in jail. I heard Joyce Meyer once say, "When you choose not to forgive the other person, it's like taking poison and hoping they get sick!" As long as you hold on to your anger, your right to be right, or your sense of being wronged, you are under the power of that anger. Chances are, the other person hasn't given it another moment's thought. So forgive them for your sake and get on with the rest of your life. Why should you lose another moment? You deserve better than that!

THE IMAGE WE SEE

This goes back to how you see yourself. In the movie *The Lion King*, the young Simba is heir to the throne of his father, who was killed. Simba thought he was to blame and accepts banishment from the land.[8] He spends the next few years living in exile with shame and low self-esteem. Turns out, he wasn't to blame at all.

Rafiki, a baboon, approaches Simba and says, "I know your father."

"My father is dead," answers Simba.

"Nope! He's alive. I'll show him to you." Rafiki the baboon leads Simba to a pool of clear water. "Look down there."

First Simba sees his own reflection, then the face of his father.

"You see, he lives in you!" says Rafiki.

Simba hears a familiar voice call his name. He looks up. His father's ghostlike image appears among the stars.

"Look inside yourself..." says the apparition. "You must take your place in the circle of life. Remember who you are..." The vision fades.

Empowered by a new sense of identity, Simba races back to Pride Rock to challenge his wicked uncle, win the throne, and restore the land. All ends well for Simba when he reclaims his true identity.

The real question comes down to how you see yourself. What image do you carry of yourself on the inside? This is important to answer because although you may well present a different image to the world, you will be hard-pressed to rise above the image you carry of yourself. A negative self-image is a form of pathogen that will stunt your growth, limit your fruit, and shorten your season of favor when it comes.

In the rainforest, infectious diseases are caused by living microorganisms called pathogens. Three critical factors or conditions must exist for disease to occur. You must have:

1 **A susceptible host plant.** A susceptible host has a genetic makeup that permits the development of a particular disease. For disease to occur, the host plant must be at a stage of development that allows it to be susceptible to infection. Plants are most susceptible to disease when they're young, when they're old, and when they're wounded.

Just like plants, we are most vulnerable when very young, very old, and when we've been emotionally wounded. If, as a child, you're told you will never amount to anything, that lie will carry a lot of weight with you and influence your development. Most of the fears we have we pick up when we're young. Childhood is a wonderful thing, but an awful lot of folks were injected with pathogens like lies, fears, wounds, and low self-image. Those who have experienced a broken marriage, betrayal, grief, or other emotional loss are also quite vulnerable to self-image problems, wounds, and unforgiveness, all of which, if not addressed and healed, will stunt or warp future growth.

2 **A pathogen.** A pathogen must be at a certain stage of development. Every disease has a contagious period.

The same is true for bad attitudes, fears, and lies. Sometimes they catch on and other times they don't.

③ Right mix of environmental conditions.
Moisture, temperature, wind, sunlight, nutrition, and soil quality affect plant growth. If one of these factors is out of balance for the culture of a specific plant, that plant may have a greater tendency to become diseased. In business and personal terms, simply put, stress makes you vulnerable to disease, be that physical, emotional, or spiritual. Keep your life in balance and actively pursue peace. The dividends will make you healthy, wealthy, and wise!

DISEASE CYCLE

In order to deal with pathogens that lurk within and hold us back, it helps to understand the five-stage process in the disease cycle.

① Inoculation. The plant must be introduced to the pathogen by wind, rain, insects, birds, or animals. The lesson to take from this is that most pathogens find you. They may come like the wind from out of nowhere and just settle on you. It could come like the driving rain with hurtful information. A pest may be the bearer of bad news, or it could be a friend or confidant. You can't stop them from coming, but you can choose how to deal with them.

② Incubation. The pathogen changes or grows into a form that can enter the new host plant. This is key because when the thought carrying the hurtful message comes to your mind, there is a time of consideration and pondering before it gains entrance. At this stage, you are considering the message, meditating on the claims, and instead of bringing that thought captive and taking your mind elsewhere, you let it incubate. And incubation leads to...

3 Penetration. Penetration typically happens through wounds or natural pores. The destructive message enters through wounds but also through natural openness. When we are young, we are more likely to believe anything said to us. We tend to be naturally open and thus vulnerable to people with ill intention.

4 Infection. The pathogen begins to grow within the plant, damaging the tissue. The lie or the fear, or whatever the pathogen is, starts preoccupying the mind and affecting your emotions and disposition.

5 Symptoms. As the pathogen consumes nutrients, the plant reacts by showing symptoms. Symptoms include mottling, dwarfing, distortion, discoloration, wilting, and shriveling of any plant part. As resources are drawn down, performance is spotty, productivity is reduced, perspective becomes distorted and unreasonable, attitude is colored, posture is slumped, and you become withdrawn.

Here's an example of how one nasty pest carrying a virus of a message affected me for years to come, much like a mosquito with malaria might cause lasting damage to any victim.

Inoculation

At the age of about eight years old, I was on the school playground at recess. As I made my way back into class, some smart-mouth kid whom I did not know and never saw again stopped me in my tracks, looked me in the eye, said, "You're ugly!" and then walked away into the crowd of other kids.

Incubation

When I got home that day, I stood in front of the hallway mirror and stared at myself for probably twenty minutes, deeply considering his words. As those words incubated in my heart and mind, I thought of all the ramifications of being ugly. In my eight-year-old mind, I assumed I would never have a girlfriend, never get married, and never have a family. I stood there pondering it all, grieved it as best I could, then accepted my fate, and never looked back.

Penetration

This didn't enter through a wound, but rather through natural, innocent openness. His words gained penetration because, in my naiveté, I assumed these were the words of an honest onlooker who felt compelled to inform me of what must be obvious to everyone else.

Infection

The damage that it did to my self-confidence, especially around the opposite sex, was very real. I assumed it was true and acted accordingly.

Symptoms

During my teen years I was very insecure with the opposite sex, and it wasn't until I met and married Brenda that I found out I wasn't ugly after all. I may not be the prize bull, but I am no longer inhibited or embarrassed by my appearance. It was amazing to me how one stray comment from a total stranger when I was a kid could impact me well into my adult years. Just think if it was a message pounded into you daily by an authority figure. Some of you know exactly what I am speaking of. It will take longer to be free from those lies.

DISEASE DEFENSE

There are three primary ways to prevent pathogens (negative, harmful messages) from gaining a foothold in your life.

 Physical characteristics. In nature, waxy or fuzzy leaf surfaces can keep pathogens at bay. For you and me, this speaks of maintaining optimal physical health. When you are physically fit, you are less prone to emotional attack. Take lots of walks, jog if you can, but be active and eat healthy.

2 **Chemical characteristics.** In nature, plants produce enzymes that kill pathogens. There are very specific actions to counter the inner battle. Offer resistance. Give it no quarter. Do not let it incubate. If a plant has a pathogen, it may also deprive it of enzymes it needs to survive. This speaks of depriving the negative input of what it needs to live, namely your approval to meditate on it and/or to talk about it. Give it no life. Deprive it of vitality.

3 **Growth patterns.** In nature, some plants will simply block off diseased tissue from contact with the rest of the plant, and it drops off. Simply put, where possible, cut off all contact with harmful sources of negative, life-destroying input in your life. The other growth pattern used by plants is to simply outgrow the damage. For you and me, that means to not let a wound stop your growth. Just keep growing despite the wound. Get past the damage.

WHEN TRIALS LEAD TO FRUITFULNESS

I recently returned from the oldest protected rainforest in the world. It's located on the island of Tobago. Only one island (Trinidad) lies between it and Venezuela, and it's believed that it once was part of the South American continent. Due to a devastating hurricane that ravaged the island in 1963 that reduced much of the ancient growth to a pile of timber, there were very few primary growth trees left. However, the lesson I learned there forever impacted me.

As my guide was taking me through the old forest trail that had been used by the tribal inhabitants of the land for time immemorial to traverse the island, it began to rain. Over the next few hours, it would start and stop repeatedly. My guide explained that this rainforest was largely fed by orographic rains. He went on to explain that much of the rain that fell was carried in by the northeast trade winds in the form of fluffy white clouds that would try to rise above the mountainous landscape and, in the process, drop their heavy rain drops, producing, in effect, an orographic rainforest.

What struck me about this was that days earlier, we were in Curacao in the Dutch Antilles. Unlike Tobago, it is a dry, desertlike island with very little topography. It hit me that the same winds blow over Curacao carrying the same clouds, but in the case of Curacao, they just pass over without dropping much of their precious cargo of rain.

Upon whom does the rain fall? The rain falls upon that terrain that puts a demand on the cloud. Now follow this with me. Think of yourself for a moment as an island. See your terrain as a picture of the circumstances in your life. Some people have rather flat, boring lives with very little rain. It may be sunny, but their lives produce very little fruitfulness.

Others have difficult, mountainous terrain, a life full of trials or obstacles. Just as the island with the mountains makes demand upon the clouds above to drop their rain, so often does the life with difficult or challenging terrain (circumstances) make demand upon God above to drop His wisdom, His words of comfort upon the soil of the heart. As a result, the island with the tough terrain gets most of the rain and produces an abundance of rich vegetation and great wealth. Similarly, the lives with the greatest trials that choose to cry out to a power higher than themselves (the Creator of both the island and the storm) oftentimes produces the richest lives and the most helpful to others.

Think about it. When have you learned the most? Was it when everything was going along fine, or when you suffered through a great trial? Though I don't yearn for the trials, I recognize that when they come, it's a great opportunity for rain. It's a great opportunity for me to grow beyond anything possible under normal circumstances. What are you going through right now? Think of your current rough terrain as a great opportunity to make a demand upon the cloud to drop down everything you need to produce fruitfulness in your life.

Mountains were formed through violent upheavals through the course of history, often erupting as a volcano, releasing a hellish inferno from deep beneath the earth. In response to the disrupted landscape, the wind, analogous to God's Spirit, brings the clouds, a picture of His presence across the landscape of your life. When those trials come, there also comes a way of getting through them. That way leads to abundance in your soul.

I mentioned earlier how I came to terms with my daughter being born with Down syndrome. As I worked through this reality, I realized that the gaping hole in my soul for her could either become a bitter pond or a well of life to help others. I chose the latter.

I made a demand upon the "cloud" to drop its "rain" and then channeled that water to nourish the seeds of faith and hope previously deposited in my heart. My heart was warmed by the presence of the cloud and nourished by the rain it left behind, and my life began to take on great abundance. To be clear with you at this moment, I must tell you that I am not speaking of financial abundance. I am speaking of an inner condition of life and abundance that would one day lead to outer abundance in any endeavor I set my hands to. Without that inner abundance, my life would never have produced an outer abundance.

So learn from the mountainous rainforests that difficult circumstances are your ticket to all the provision you need to prepare you for great abundance, if you make demand upon the cloud and receive the rain of wisdom, comfort, knowledge, and insight just floating above your head.

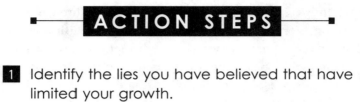

1 Identify the lies you have believed that have limited your growth.

2 What is the truth?

3 What is your biggest fear?

4 What information or action can turn away that fear?

5 What pains have been inflicted upon you that you have not let go of?

6 Let go of them now. Forgive that person now.

7 What image do you hold of yourself?

8 What is the image you believe you were intended to carry?

WEALTH SECRET #4

THE PHOTOSYNTHESIS OF IDEAS
Turning Vision Into Provision

It is not the critic who counts, not the man who points
out how the strong man stumbled, or where the doer of
deeds could have done better. The credit belongs to the
man who is actually in the arena; whose face is marred by
the dust and sweat and blood; who strives valiantly; who
errs and comes short again and again; who knows the
great enthusiasms, the great devotions and spends himself
in a worthy course; who at the best, knows in the end the
triumph of high achievement, and who, at worst, if he
fails, at least fails while daring greatly; so that his place
shall never be with those cold and timid souls who know
neither victory or defeat.[1]

TEDDY ROOSEVELT

AFTER SPEAKING AT AN INVESTMENT SEMINAR IN BELIZE, MY
wife and I hired a driver and invited our dear friend Joe Johnson,
another presenter at that event, to head off for a few days and
explore the only English-speaking country in Central America. Belize
is a beautiful country with lovely beaches, lush countryside, and, of
course, some tropical rainforest as well. The thing that struck me as
we drove up the coast and later on up through the Maya Mountain

range in this resource-rich country was the complete lack of vision. Most homes were in disrepair or only half built. I saw nothing done with excellence except the resort hotels by the beaches. It amazed me that a country so rich in resources, so blessed with beautiful climate, so abundant in natural provision would see itself in such a slovenly light.

If you think it's just that they are a poor, third-world country, I would disagree. They are a rich country. They just have a poor mind-set, limited vision, and very little drive. If Belize was a client of mine and I could help them run it like a company, it wouldn't be long before we were lifting the national malaise, working fruitfully, and turning a profit that would be shared with stakeholders proportionate to their contribution. Certainly there are exceptions, and the people I met in Belize were kind and gentle people, but they were living so far below their capacity. It was sad. Their collective countenance was what you might expect to see on the faces of the last place high school basketball team after they were routed by the second from last place team at the end of another losing season! Their eyes were open, but there was no light on inside.

Stepping in to fill the void are Europeans, Americans, Asians, and many others who come to Belize to build for themselves the life originally offered to and intended for the beautiful people of Belize. What Belize and other countries like it need are the same things a successful company needs—the will and ability to transform intangible vision (dreams) into tangible, physical reality. From my limited perspective, the Belizeans could readily see the vision of others taking shape, and, no doubt, many wanted to live that dream themselves but counted themselves out, due to perceived lack of finances or know-how. Whether you lack vision and have talent or lack talent but have vision, either way the most you can hope for is to see your dreams float by you like a cloud in the summer sky unless you do something about it! That's why I wrote this book and, in particular, this chapter!

As you already know from reading the chapter on growing toward the light, sunlight powers the rainforest, but without the process of photosynthesis there would be no life on the planet. Photosynthesis is the process of combining light energy, water, and CO_2 to produce chemical energy in the form of carbohydrates (food). Just how it does that is not so simple to understand, and you will be hard-pressed to find two Web sites that describe this process in exactly the same way. I have probably spent more time researching this amazing process than I have actually spent in the rainforest observing it! It's imperative that you understand this process in business terms if you really want to turn the intangible into tangible and make a profit doing so.

Think about this. The wooden furniture in your home used to be a tree in the forest. Before that it was a sapling, and before that it was a seed. Before that it was nowhere! The cake I wish I was eating right now with my second cup of coffee outside in our lanai used to be separate components of flour, sugar, butter, and whatever else they put in cakes. But wood is really the product of light, water, and air. How plants do that is amazing! They, in effect, turn water into wine (if they're a grapevine) every day! It's a miracle in slow speed so you can observe it and learn from it.

In business, the photosynthesis of ideas is the process of focusing vision (light energy), information (water), and effort (CO_2) on a single goal to achieve a desired result. It sounds simple, but there's more. Photosynthesis has two stages with a total of seven steps that convert light energy into sustenance. When you look at how the process works, you begin to see a pretty exciting business model anyone can adopt.

The photosynthesis of ideas is the process of receiving and spreading vision, setting goals and objectives, leveraging accumulated understanding to formulate a plan (guided by principle), and then assigning the right people possessing the right strengths to work consistently on the action steps according to the practices (habits), policies, and procedures given. It consists of two stages: visioning or planning stage, and the implementation stage where resources are spent on actualizing the vision. It breaks down like this:

Step	The Science	The Application
Step 1	Capture the light	Capture the vision
Step 2	Electrons energize others	Spread the vision
Step 3	Enzymes break down H_2O	Leaders develop a plan
Step 4	Hydrogen energizes molecules	Team defines next steps
Step 5	Hydrogen and CO_2 combine	Work begins
Step 6	½ glucose passes through chloroplasts	Individual results evaluated
Step 7	Food produced and distributed	Project comes together

—STAGE ONE—

LIGHT-DEPENDENT STAGE: VISION REFINEMENT STAGE

The science

The purpose of leaves is quite simple; they make food for the whole plant. Since their entire function is to trap light energy and convert it to chemical energy, everything in a leaf is constructed and arranged with that idea in mind.

The application

The purpose of a business is quite simple; it is to provide a product or service to serve a target market. Since the purpose is then to convert the vision of the leader into a visible reality providing value all around, everything in a company should be constructed and arranged with that idea in mind.

Step #1

The science—chloroplasts capture the light

Chloroplasts acting like antennae capture light energy from the sun to produce the free energy stored in ATP and NADPH through a process called photosynthesis.

The application—capture the vision

For the vision to be captured, it must get out of the founder's head and into a format that can be read, reviewed and shared. Write it out; make it clear and compelling.

Step #2

The science—electrons get excited and energize others

When light photons hit chlorophyll electrons, one electron is knocked loose, gets excited (higher state of being energized), and goes dancing off to provide the energy, motivation, and excitement to start the photosynthesis process. Light appears to travel as either a wave or a particle, depending on how you happen to be looking at it. When it travels as a particle, the little particles of energy are called photons.

The application—spread the vision

Once the vision has been captured, it must be shared far and wide throughout the organization. This is not a one-time occurrence. It is part of the normal dialogue of the company. When vision is ignited, energy is released. Emotion, motivation, and inspiration are knocked loose and begin to affect others in the organization.

Step #3

The science—enzymes break down water into usable form

Simultaneous to the light energy traveling through the plant, a special enzyme breaks apart the water molecules that have entered the plant from the roots into hydrogen and oxygen. (Enzymes are protein molecules that make things happen. During photosynthesis they grab various atoms and molecules and move them and assemble them into new molecules. *Each assembly step requires a unique enzyme to perform it.*)

The application—key individuals in the organization break down the information into an actionable plan

The vision is great. It's the feel-good part, but we need a road map or instruction manual guiding us through the process of materializing the vision. This is where your leadership team working with key agents in the company determines the goals, specific objectives, realistic time frames, and unambiguous benchmarks along the way. A written plan is formulated based on accumulated in-house knowledge, and guiding principles for decision making are agreed upon.

Goals

The French philosopher and priest Geoffrey F. Abert (1079–1142) famously said, "The most important thing about goals is having one."[2] Goals are broad, general, intangible, and worthwhile. They have the power to inspire others while stretching you. If they don't stretch you, they're not goals; they're tasks. Wes Cantrell, former CEO of Harris 3M and Lanier Worldwide, shared a great example of an inspiring goal that the team came up with to set their company apart. It was the late 1980s, and, after measuring their customer satisfaction rate, they discovered they were on par with the rest of the copier industry with about a 47 percent satisfaction rate.[3] They made it their goal to be the best in customer satisfaction in the country. That was a worthwhile goal and a lofty one at that! Zig Ziglar says, "A goal properly set is halfway reached."[4]

Objectives

Peter Drucker said, "Management by objective works—if you know the objectives. Ninety percent of the time you don't."[5] Objectives are the narrow, precise, tangible, and measurable accomplishments that must be achieved for your goal to be reached. If you only know the goal and not the objectives, you will likely fail in your goal. When Wes Cantrell and his leadership team set out to be recognized as the best in customer service, as rated by actual customers, they knew they had to measure their starting point, assess their weaknesses, begin training people, work on it, and improve it incrementally. The goal was lofty, but they had specific measurable objectives along the way, which took them from 47 percent in customer satisfaction to about 94 percent in the mid-1990s. They kept improving it, and right after Wes retired, they won the prestigious JD Power Award for being the best copier company as measured by customer satisfaction in 2002 and 2003.[6] A goal without objectives is like a frog without legs. It can float, but it won't go anywhere!

Realistic time frames

Having a time frame for completion of an objective or goal creates a sense of urgency. Parkinson's Law states that work expands to fill the time allotted. The longer you allow for completion of a project, the longer it generally takes. The foundation I worked for has a goal to raise an endowment on par with the most established learning institutions in America. As an initial objective, it was determined that $100 million would be a good starting point to begin building the business school. So far, so good, but without a time frame it really didn't mean much. Sure, they wanted it right away, but that wasn't realistic. Ten years seemed a little protracted, so it was determined to grow the endowment by $100 million in a twenty-month period. With an aggressive but measurable objective, the race was on, and they closed out 2007 with an endowment value of $50 million with twelve months remaining to get the rest.

Adding a time frame and sticking with it is absolutely critical for success. When I started selling copiers in Nashville back in 1986 after moving there from Canada, I wanted to make a favorable impression on my employer and my peers and gain a leadership position. One of my objectives early on was to set a record for the most sales ever made in the first full month of employment. Their expectation was only about one copier, and they would have said nothing if there were no sales. They wanted two sales my second month and four per month thereafter.

I set my objective to make ten sales by the end of my first full month in the company. Doing so would put me well on my way to my goal of leadership in the company while shattering any previous record. By midafternoon of the last day of the month, I had only eight sales in hand with no prospects or leads for more. I called my wife on a break, and she encouraged me to celebrate the number I had achieved, which no one else had done before me in their first month. I knew she meant well, but I had to hang up from her because I was still fixated on the objective and there was still time on the clock. The fact that I had a specific number with an exact time frame propelled me back into action.

As it happened, a prospect came into our office needing a used copier of the type and model an existing customer who was considering upgrading had. Before the day was over, I assisted the new prospect in acquiring my customer's used copier (sale number nine) and then accommodated my existing customer by supplying a newer, faster, better model for his growing business (sale number ten). There were a number of factors that made that record possible, but certainly chief among them was having a specific, measurable objective *with a nonnegotiable time frame*. On the flip side, if the time frame for accomplishment was set unrealistically for my first day instead of my first month, it wouldn't have marshaled the internal resolve to get it done. An objective without a time frame is like a bird without wings. It may get to the destination, but it will probably take a lot longer!

Unambiguous benchmarks

In order to hit that goal, it was imperative that certain benchmarks were attained along the way. A certain number of presentations had to be made, preceded by a certain number of client interviews, preceded by a certain number of canvas calls, all of which had to be accomplished along the way. To realistically hit the goal of ten sales, I wanted to have some sales locked up by midmonth, a couple more by the end of the third week, then a steady stream of business the last week.

Whether we are talking about sales objectives, production objectives, marketing objectives, and so forth, it is very instructive to set benchmarks along the way. Otherwise you will get to the end of the agreed-upon time frame and only then find out whether you succeeded or not. It's too late! Benchmarks help you make course corrections. They are like lighthouses along a rocky shore. They alert you to danger and point you to safety. Time frames without benchmarks is like sailing in the fog. You never know whether you're doing well or failing miserably until it's too late.

Written plan

Earl Nightingale said, "Your problem is to bridge the gap which exists between where you are now and the goal you intend to reach."[7] As Alan Lakein once commented, "Planning is bringing the future into the present so that you can do something about it now."[8] A well-executed plan beats flying by the seat of your pants anytime. It begins with the vision-aligned goal and spells out the objectives, time frames, and benchmarks, but it also answers the who, what, where, and how, laying out the succession of events that must occur to reach the goal.

Guiding principles

These are the core values by which decisions are made. You can't anticipate every scenario and have a planned response written for it in the employee handbook. At Selling Among Wolves, we adapted seven guiding principles to our business so that anyone faced with a difficult customer situation, for example, could refer to guiding principles by which we operate to help them make a decision. Here's what we use:

 Just: Before engaging in any activity or recommending a course of action, we will ask, "Is it just?"

 True: When we speak, write, or advertise, we will ask, "Is it true?"

Peace: We will strive to bring peace to our customer's storms. We will strive to walk in peace.

 Good: We will strive for excellence in all we do.

 Agreeable: We will work to find agreement quickly with our vendors, clients, and prospects.

 Mercy: We will walk in mercy toward others, giving the benefit of the doubt, forgiving wrongs quickly.

 Everlasting: We will strive to deliver consistent quality reliably over the long term.

Step #4

The science—hydrogen ions energize molecules that do the work

The hydrogen ions go zipping out of the hydrogen reservoir where they were temporarily stored and provide energy for the production of ATP and NADPH (two energy-carrying molecules that power the dark reactions).

The application—supervisors (leaders) get with workers to define next steps

This is where the plan is broken down into the step-by-step expectations of each person involved. Every team member at every level must know and understand in this step exactly how they contribute to the vision and how they will be measured. The first step is to identify what Eric Beck (www.totalintegrationnow.com) calls "anchor activities." These are the tasks you must do daily or weekly or even monthly to do your job. They may include responding to e-mails, making customer calls, answering inbound calls, attending staff meetings, or performing production review. Be sure that the process for accomplishing those anchor activities is agreed upon and in writing. Provide training and the necessary tools for success. Agree on individual projects that are not part of the anchor activity list but need to get done, and include respective time frames, benchmarks, and action steps for completion.

Metrics are agreed upon at this stage. This is critical. Everyone must know what it takes for them to succeed. Decide what will be measured. There are internal metrics, which typically includes two things: input and output—or, to say it another way: activity and result, actions and outcomes. You should measure both the effort and the result. At this point, you introduce rewards and sanctions—rewards for rising above a certain level and sanctions for falling below an acceptable level. If there is no consequence or reward for doing the work, you establish that it doesn't really matter if you do it. Base compensation at some level upon hitting certain activity levels. If their activity level is low, it doesn't merit the same reward that a hardworking team member receives. Pay for accomplishment, not time.

Other important factors to measure are customer satisfaction markers. This can be done by survey, callback rates, complaints, or compliments. The business exists to serve the customer, so getting a measurement on that is very important. A customer is anyone, whether internal or external, who receives whatever product or service is produced by the company or by an individual in the line of one's duties that has value. Being customer-centered means that you leverage assets and skills at your disposal on behalf of the customer to meet the needs you are contracted to fulfill in a way that exceeds their expectations and assists in reaching their goals. Identify the profile of internal and external customers and agree on standards of quality and performance, then measure those.

The more people know about their job, their customers, your product or service, the industry, and so on, the better they can serve the whole. At the foundation I served, people in certain positions are tested for knowledge and measured for growth in those areas. Set performance standards in the learning or continuous education department as well. When your team hits those standards, not only does their value increase to you, but also the corporate value increases to the customer.

Last but not least, where possible, monetize the value of their anchor activities and project completion. Measure top-line contribution, expense, and bottom-line delivery. Financial metrics are an important part of the total metrics needed, so include them in every job function you can.

In order for metrics to work fairly and be relevant, these seven questions should be answered in advance:

1 What is being measured?

2 How will it be measured?

3 Who will measure it?

4 What is the unit of measurement?

5 How frequently will it be measured?

6 What are the current metrics?

7 What are the target metrics?

Of course, activity is not always good enough. It must produce results. That's the other leg of the compensation plan. If people are doing the right thing, the right result will follow, and when it does, reward it as well. I recommend paying a base amount based on specific minimum activity. If they accomplish more, then bonus accordingly. Allow people to attain above-average income if they also produce results above a certain benchmark. Bonus exceptional results exceptionally.

—STAGE TWO—

LIGHT-INDEPENDENT STAGE: VISION IMPLEMENTATION STAGE

Step #5

The science—hydrogen meets CO_2 to form ½ glucose molecule

A bunch of different enzymes use the carbon dioxide molecules and hydrogen ions made during the light-dependent phase to assemble sugar fragments, which are half of a glucose molecule. (CO_2 is captured and modified by the addition of hydrogen to form half a glucose molecule.)

The application—plans meet with effort to produce results (rubber meets the road)

In the valley of indecision and inaction lie the skeletal remains of many a worthy plan. The time for talk is over. Theorizing and speculating, dreaming and planning are done. This is the activity stage, where effort meets skill and the shoulder is put to the plow. It's time to get to work! I love what Lebanese artist Khalil Gibran's perspective on work is: "Work is love made visible."[9] Thomas Carlyle adds, "Work alone is noble."[10] My wife simply says, "Talk's cheap!"

Perhaps Thomas Edison said it the most pragmatically when he stated, "Being busy does not always mean real work. The object of all work is production or accomplishment and to either of these ends there must be forethought, system, planning, intelligence, and honest purpose, as well as perspiration."[11] Diligence must now be offered to the plan or it will fail.

It seems that people would rather talk than work, but Solomon said that talk only leads to poverty. Set the standard high and monitor progress. Hold folks accountable for very short-term results at first. If you have an in-house sales team whose job it is to make outbound calls and secure business, you might have to begin by setting expectations for the first hour of the day, or possibly every hour of the day. The point is to set in place good work habits. Once the habits have been ingrained, you can back off the micromanagement, but until good habits are established, don't expect what you don't inspect!

Step #6

The science—the ½-glucose molecules must pass through chloroplasts

The next step for the half-glucose molecules is to pass through the chloroplasts outer membrane into the cell. That's where more enzymes work together to join the 3-carbon fragments with another 3-carbon fragment and produce sugar (glucose).

The application

The results must pass through the vision inspection. Before rewarding the team members for their contribution, results must be measured against expectations, against the vision, and against what was possible. This is where we look for and measure result. Has the hard work paid off? Did our efforts produce food? This is the culmination of everything we've planned and worked for. We now count the harvest, share the reward, or sanction non-performers. Sanction may simply consist of moving them to an area better suited for them where they can excel.

Step #7

The science—the glucose becomes the basic building block for a number of other carbohydrates, such as sucrose, lactose, ribose, cellulose, and starch

They can then move on into other plant cells. Of course, if the leaf gets eaten, the energy gets transferred into animal cells. From there they can be used to make fats, oils, amino acids, and proteins.

The application—completed individual goals allow the project to come together

Finished parts may become a whole. My wife and I wrote a book years ago, called *Psalm 91—The Ultimate Shield*, for her son being shipped off to the Persian Gulf in the first Gulf war.[12] We only had a short time to complete and publish the book before he left Camp Lejeune, North Carolina, for the Middle East. Mark Herron, our highly talented graphic artist in Atlanta (www.mrherron.com), began designing the cover. We began writing the book while our staff lined up a typesetter and a printer made room in their schedule. The book came together like magic and was in Camp Lejeune just three weeks after Scott got the call to head out.

Photosynthesis is the science of business lived out in front of us every day. Applying a natural, scientific approach to business assures a greater chance for success. Science still has a lot to learn about this process we call photosynthesis, and we all have a lot to learn about the science of business and the management of household things (economics). Visit our Web site (www.RainforestStrategy.com) to find more resources to help you integrate these steps into your business. Consider joining us and other leading experts for a rainforest expedition that will not only make for a great vacation but will also help you succeed in business.

ACTION STEPS

1 What are the goals and time frames included in your vision?

2 What are the specific objectives, with time frames, required to realize your vision?

3 What are the benchmarks you must reach (and when) to accomplish your goals and objectives?

4 Develop a written plan with all goals, objectives, and benchmarks figured in.

5 Identify your core guiding principles.

6 What metrics will you use to track your progress?

■　■　■　■

WEALTH SECRET #5

THE STRANGLER FIG PHENOMENON
A Lesson in Timing

> To every thing there is a season, and a time for every purpose under the heaven.... A time to plant, and a time to pluck up that which is planted.[1]
>
> KING SOLOMON

> And he shall be like a tree planted by the rivers of water that bringeth forth his fruit in his season; his leaf also shall not wither; and whatsoever he doeth shall prosper.[2]
>
> KING DAVID

THE STRANGLER FIG, LIKE ALL PLANTS, GOES THROUGH FOUR distinct phases over the course of its life, but so do people, businesses, economies, and nations. Life is a cycle, and the four seasons of the year are but a microcosm of the larger cycles we often fail to see. Have you ever seen a bright rainbow in the sky and then looked a little further out and seen a second or even a third rainbow, increasingly bigger and harder to see? I've seen as many as three at one time. Most people see the first one, but the successive rainbows, called supernumerary rainbows, are often visible as well, but because they are further out and much fainter, they are often missed.

Like multiple rainbows, there are also multiple cycles of life, all of them having a direct bearing on what happens to your business. Discerning the seasons in each cycle and planning accordingly can make a huge difference in the success of your company. Would you have wanted to open up a new manufacturing plant in 1910 to produce buggy whips when the horseless carriage was coming on the scene? Would you plant corn in September just because it was sunny and warm? If not, then read this chapter carefully and discern the seasons of life and business.

THE SHORT CYCLE

This is the easy one. Everyone recognizes winter, spring, summer, and fall. It's an annual cycle caused by the tilt of the earth's rotational axis away from or toward the sun as it travels through its yearlong path around the sun. In every culture, each season has special holidays commemorating some special historical event. The short cycle in business looks like this:

- **Design (seed time):** You come up with a new idea for a product. That may be a description of an information product, a prototype of a physical product, a drawing of a new house design, or a pattern for a new part.

- **Build (plant—invest):** Once you are satisfied the design has merit and the new product will succeed, you enter into production. For information products, that means writing, recording, duplicating, and loading onto a Web site.

- **Market (grow demand):** Marketing the new design typically occurs when the product is ready to ship, but we have done well letting the seasons overlap a bit. When we had the idea for our first-ever audio coaching program for sales, it consisted of twelve one-hour audio programs plus a four-page written summary for each module. Back then, recording time in studio was a big investment for us, as was the entire manufacturing process of thousands of cassettes with thousands of four-color curriculum sheets and a very handsome storage binder that contained it all.

To help with cash-flow considerations, we did a prelaunch promotion promising delivery in four to six weeks. There were a bunch of people who wanted to be the first to get our unique teaching program for sales. As a result, the marketing was a big success for us with enough pre-orders to cover all production costs and get us firmly launched in the information marketing business.

- **Sell (harvest time):** Sales follow marketing. Sometimes, if the marketing is direct response, the sales are immediate, but oftentimes the marketing generates leads that must be followed up on.

Every time you have a new design, you go through the same four seasons. The more successful companies I have worked with have this down to such a science that after a design or new product concept has been approved, different teams are assigned to each phase and they work synchronously so there's no lag time between each season.

BUSINESS LESSON #1

Create promotions for your product or service in sync with seasonal events. That's obvious to retailers, and they never miss the chance to put on a sale, be that Christmas, after Christmas, New Year's, Valentine's Day, or back to school—but it works well in many other businesses as well. Besides the Rainforest Institute, I also have a sales training and consulting firm called Selling Among Wolves. With my consulting schedule booked out far into the future, I have chosen to make the information my clients want most available via download, CD, DVD, books, newsletter, or podcasts. They are in no way seasonal, but I have found that my customers enjoy the special offers we make at those times, and we certainly enjoy the increased revenue.

In 2008 we had a leap year, and for the first time ever, I heard the term "leap day." It sounded catchy to me, so that very same day, February 29, we sent out our first ever Leap Day promotion, which we vowed not to offer again until 2012. Customers loved the story we told and the offer we presented. That gave us a nice bonus that day. Going forward, we plan on tying promotions in to just about every high-profile day of the year. Don't worry that your product or service has nothing to do with the season. Make the offer compelling and give folks that extra reason to purchase now.

THE LONG CYCLE

This cycle lasts a life span regardless of whether we are speaking of the life span of a plant, a tree, or a human. With that cycle, there tends to be four seasons. With people, it can be categorized as infancy, youth, adult, old age, or, as I read recently, (1) you believe in Santa Claus, (2) you don't believe in Santa Claus, (3) you are Santa Claus, and (4) you look like Santa Claus!

In the rainforest, the cycle of life progresses through four stages as well, and they speak very strongly to business. Kiuchi and Shireman, in *What We Learned in the Rainforest*, conclude, "Businesses, like forests and all complex systems, tend to evolve through four life phases.... At any moment, different elements of the business will be in different phases. In each phase, current performance is maximized through dramatically different and often-competing success factors. Future performance—and the sustainability of the business itself—is enhanced by developing the success factors of the next phase, even at the cost of the current one. The sustainability imperative is that, in any one phase, a living system must master the success factors of the next phase in order to be sustainable."[3]

Knowing which phase your business is in will help you anticipate and plan for the next one. Each phase requires different competencies that, if you don't acquire them, you will not graduate to the next level. The sad thing is, you may never know why. The four phases go by different names, but all contain a similar meaning. They are innovation, growth, maturity, and release.

PHASE I—INNOVATION

The difference between creativity and innovation is that innovation requires action while creativity requires only thought. Innovation is about implementing the creative idea. The idea must become tangible and provide meaningful value. Think of the innovation stage in business as the start-up phase. The goal here is fruitfulness. Before fruitfulness, businesses in this phase generally require substantial investment of time, talent, and treasure to create the customer base and business model that is self-sustaining. The innovation stage is typically high risk and low profit. The model, however, must work before going to the next level.

You see innovators in the rainforest when a big tree goes down and opens up a gap for light to penetrate the forest floor. Shrubs, saplings, and some grasses live for such a day. They grow toward the light and compete for control of the ground area or soil (capital). If the grass gets there first and controls a large enough area, a tree can never get a foothold. On the other hand, if a tree has a good start, it can eventually provide enough shade and capture enough light to starve the grass of its energy source, eventually causing the grass to die and yield its organic compounds to the root system of the tree.

When the World Wide Web opened up, it was like a clearing opening in the rainforest. Only it wasn't the same as a single tree going down; it was more like a logging operation had gone through. Vast access to wide-open territory had provided opportunities for new industries, new ways of doing old things, and all over the world there were dot-com millionaires in their twenties. In one sense it opened the playing field so innovators could come in who had no prior business experience. They didn't have to own an established business to play. In fact, most of them didn't.

Before I had a Web site or an e-mail address, I received a call from one of those twenty-something entrepreneurs who had heard me on the radio and wanted to hire me for a three-day consulting project to help him grow his new business. This young man, Scott Sanders, who later became a dear friend, had an idea to auction cattle on the Internet and called his company Cyber Stockyard. I was well behind the innovation curve that was happening and watched with amazement how he and his team of equally young entrepreneurs and one smart investor turned that idea into a thriving success, selling in a very short time for several million dollars! While others were trying to figure out if the World Wide Web was going to affect their business, innovators like Scott Sanders were moving in and taking territory!

In the rainforest, innovators take control of territory (ground space) very seriously, and the competition for those capital resources (soil) can even turn deadly. There is an Asian grass that was introduced to Panama in about 1970 known as paja grass. The grass itself is quite productive, but it tends to crowd out other plants that want to share the land with it. During the dry season, paja grass dries out considerably, providing fuel for fire, when lightning strikes, that literally destroys its competitors while somehow managing to survive the flames itself.

While on Barro Colorado Island, I was fortunate enough to pick up the book *A Magic Web* with wonderfully vivid photos by Christian Zieglar and thoughtful, easy-to-understand text by Egbert Giles Leigh Jr. In that book, Egbert explains in business terms the forces at work in the rainforest. He writes:

> Ecosystems, like economies, are webs of interdependence. Each species depends in many ways on the ecological context in which it evolved, just as a business firm depends on its economic or social context. Disrupt the context, and most suffer.
>
> Indeed, ecosystems resemble economies more than they do organisms. Like economies, ecosystems are both arenas of competition and conflict, and functional systems with a mutually beneficial division of labor among their participants. Not only is there division of labor among producers, consumers, and decomposers; there is division of labor among producers adapted to different stations in the forest—canopy trees, understory trees, ground-herbs, and so forth. Likewise, there is a division of labor among organisms that decompose dead matter of different kinds—indeed, among those involved in different stages of decomposing each kind. Pollinators and seed dispersers maintain a tropical forest's productivity by allowing its trees to escape excessive herbivory without overloading themselves with growth-reducing antiherbivore toxins. Such diversity of function does enhance the forest's productivity.
>
> Competition is the driving force behind this division of labor. A species that exploits a source of energy available to a community better than any already present can establish itself if it reaches that community. Competition, however, is sometimes destructive. Paja grass spreads by providing fuel for fires

that burn up its competitors. On the other hand, the success of destructive competition may be ephemeral. If destructive competition leaves resources grossly underused, something will evolve to exploit them. More generally, a species that makes its living in ways that benefit the most other species and harm the fewest is least liable to the evolution of counter measures by adversely affected species.[4]

The innovation stage of a business is much like the innovation stage of a leaf when it first emerges from the branch. It's not rigid and tough, but rather soft and supple, allowing it to grow quickly, unhindered by rigid cell structures that limit growth. An innovator in business has not yet become hardened and stuck in his ways. This allows him to rapidly adjust to fluctuating market conditions and take over new ground (opportunities) before the older established businesses have completed their initial SWOT assessment of the same opportunity. (That's assuming they even saw it in the first place!)

Richard Foster and Sarah Kaplan, authors of *Creative Destruction*, point out, "During the 20th century, highly revered and much-touted 'built to last' corporations tended to underperform the market by a significant amount, while upstarts outperformed the market and their established competitors." Just like leaves thicken up and toughen up, they contend, "As corporations grow and become more complex, they become weighed down by rules and procedures that discourage innovation.... Organizations seeking to succeed, not just survive, must learn to 'act like the market' and adopt policies that will enable them to 'change at the pace and scale of the market.'"[5]

Innovators are also the most vulnerable due to their rapid consumption of resources during the start-up phase and the high visibility they can create if successful. I have one client right now who would be celebrated in business magazines across the country for their success if they were to release their financials, but they decline the prestige to avoid attracting other competitors. They are keeping a low profile like the paja grass and grabbing a lot of vacant territory at the moment. By the time other innovators catch on or the establishment notices, they will be a formidable force indeed. As they approach that time, they will have to continue to innovate to avoid becoming like some of the other slow-moving, self-congratulating behemoths in their industry. As Foster and Kaplan suggest, "Companies that do achieve returns that are above the industry average are likely to be new entrants that enjoy superior performance only for a limited time; they surprise analysts, whose historical models cannot adequately forecast their performance. And, they generate high investor return, only to inevitably fall into more normal patterns of corporate behavior and industry and market performance." They contend, "Strong long-term performance can only be achieved by mastering continual change."[6]

Even the nonprofit foundation I assisted is an innovator. Their endowment-building strategy is a big success, and they are expanding rapidly. As an innovator going for the open ground, they know it will be contested. While others debate the viability of the opportunity, they are taking territory. Rapid growth means rapid consumption of resources, but if you have the right innovation and can sustain cash flow, rapid growth is a great strategy to keep out the competition. In the rainforest, growth is fueled by light. In business, innovation is fueled by vision. When others see your innovation, they will catch some of the light and compete with you for territory. The longer you can maintain a low profile or the quicker you can appear to have already won the battle so as to discourage entry, the better.

Innovations come in two basic types

The first one is gradual, incremental, subtle, but continuous. It's like the incoming tide. You barely notice its approach, but you can't miss its effect. The second one is sudden, unexpected, radical, life-changing, and intermittent. It's like a tidal wave or tsunami. It arrives without notice and changes the landscape. You can't miss its approach, and you won't forget its effect. Let's start with the tsunami.

1 **Tsunami innovations** change life for almost everyone, at least eventually. First we had the wheel, then there were sharp stones for axes and arrowheads, then came the French crossbow, which was like a rifle with arrows, and the British longbow with its power,

precision, and rapid rate of fire. Automobiles, airplanes, television, telephones, computers, and the incandescent light bulb are all examples of tsunami innovations. Like tsunamis, they get a lot of press, everyone starts talking about it, and all eyes are open for the next one.

2 **Tidal innovations** are helpful and may only impact one department or one person, but if done consistently throughout the organization, they will keep it alive, vibrant, and very healthy. The innovations may be as slight as improving a form, a way of reporting, or the language in a marketing piece. Business is not static. The landscape is always changing. If you're not growing, you're dying. Better wake up to that! It's the little things that make the difference, and the process of continuous improvement can dramatically impact outcomes.

Take, for example, something as simple as a sales process. Suppose you have in your process the following key steps: contact, interview, presentation, and close. Did you know you can increase sales by over 70 percent by bringing only a 10 percent incremental improvement to six smaller parts of the process? Here's how.

Using the following hypothetical metrics, assume a 10 percent incremental increase in each step.

	Current		Plus 10 percent	
Activity	Rate	Quantity	Rate	Quantity
Calls per month	50/day	1,100	55/day	1,210
Contacts per month	20 percent	220	22 percent	266
Resulting interviews per month	30 percent	66	33 percent	88
Resulting presentations per month	50 percent	33	55 percent	48
Resulting sales per month	33 percent	11	36.3 percent	17
Average dollar value per sale	$5,000		$5,500	
Total revenue per month	$55,000		$93,500	

	Current		Plus 10 percent	
Activity	Rate	Quantity	Rate	Quantity
Total annualized revenue	$660,000		$1,122,000 + 70 percent	

A plant in the rainforest makes incremental changes as it grows—first the shoot, then the branches, and ultimately the fruit. Like the caterpillar said to the rabbit, "Inch by inch, anything's a cinch." Limits in the rainforest, however, also cause incremental changes. Take, for example, the whole debate on global warming, regardless of the cause; what we do know is that if it continues, it will gradually change life on the planet. We know, for example, that palm trees used to grow in Greenland. If it happened before, it may well happen again. The incremental changes will mean coastal flooding, new real estate becoming available while other real estate disappears, and a myriad of changes in what grows where. Costa Rica at one time had a small number of fern species, but the latest number I read was over eleven hundred variations that came upon the scene slowly, incrementally.

Tidal innovations improve what the tsunami innovation brought to us. Telephones became digital and then portable. Computers moved from the office to the home to the beach. Cars went from hand-crank starts to voice command, from burning gas to ethanol to electric and solar. The truth is, we need both types of innovation. While looking for the next tsunami innovation, if you really want to grow your business, practice consistent, like-the-tide, incremental improvement.

One last thing about the process of incremental improvement: it's kind of like compound interest in that you don't get much out of it on any day or even in any one year, but over the long haul it is simply amazing. Suppose you're twenty years old and want to retire with a million dollars. If you set aside $13,719.21 compounding at 10 percent per year today, you would have $1,000,000 set aside when you retire. Who knows what a million dollars will buy you then, but you see the point. Now let's apply that to incremental improvement. If you can bring incremental improvement at or above your rate of consumption, you will never run out. For example, if you consume one hundred gallons of heating oil for your home yearly, and you only have one thousand gallons to start with, you have a ten-year supply. During the first year, you burn up one hundred gallons, but you also figure a way to be 10 percent more efficient so that you can get the same heat from ninety gallons of oil. You start your second year with only nine hundred gallons of oil, but now you are only burning ninety gallons per year, so you still have a ten-year supply. As long as you can keep improving at a rate that matches or exceeds your consumption rate, you have a limitless supply. Logic suggests that at some point that becomes impractical, which is when you must come up with a tsunami innovation for a new source of energy.

PHASE II—GROWTH

You have the working model; now you grow it. This might mean multiple locations, additional staff, and so on. I know of Internet marketers who develop niche Web sites for unusual but beneficial products. They begin with one product and a direct-response Web site. They get it up and running and perhaps producing just a few hundred dollars per month in positive cash flow. It doesn't seem like much, but once they have a working model, they develop a new product, build a new Web site using the same marketing strategies that worked in the first one, and simply replicate their success. Some of these guys have hundreds of Web sites earning them anywhere from one hundred dollars per month to two thousand dollars per month. They develop a working model, make it fruitful, and then multiply it.

Businesses in the growth phase can often function using their own limited resources. However, rapid growth leads to rapid consumption of resources and can sometimes lead to severe cash-flow shortages and the closure of business. In a temperate forest when one species takes over a dominant position, it attracts more attention from the pests and there can be mass die-off. In the late 1980s, a spruce bark beetle epidemic began in Alaska, peaking about ten years later after killing white spruce trees on several million acres of federal and state land in the Kenai Peninsula south of Anchorage and the Copper River area east of Anchorage.[7] That will never happen in the rainforest because instead of being dominated by one or two species, it is incredibly diverse with thousands of species and no one pest or pathogen develops to any significant number focused on any one species.

When you grow rapidly in business, you attract pests, some of which are predatory and deadly, just like in the rainforest. They want you out of business. It may simply be a competitive thing or jealousy, but you have to make up your mind whether to defend against the pests, which consumes resources and slows growth, or ignore your detractors, take the hits from the pests, and try to outgrow them. Either way is a gamble, but I believe the best decision has to do with your DNA. What are you good at? If you are good at growing, then maybe you divert minimal resources to defense and keep growing. If your strength is defense, then invest there and plot your growth slowly but surely.

During the growth stage, consumer demand is established and increases. This usually means the need for extra help in every department from production to operations, sales to customer service in order to serve the growing base and to continue growing. As volume increases, some efficiencies begin to come into play, such as buying power, batching work flow, or increased productivity from new equipment that becomes affordable. All of these things work together to further increase sales and enhance profit margins.

During this time it is important to create loyalty with your customers. The investment to get a new customer far outweighs the cost of keeping an existing customer. Develop a customer loyalty program to reward customers for their loyalty. This could be a discount on future purchases, a membership with special privileges, or simply a meaningful show of gratitude that demonstrates you are not taking them for granted.

PHASE III—MATURITY

By this time, the firm is well established. It is known in the industry and respected. It has a reputation, and that reputation, if good, generates its own stream of business. Customers tend to not work you so hard for price concessions because they know the quality of the work and service you bring. You are now a proven entity that can back up your claims. In this phase the focus trends toward maintaining market share, but it needs to include plans for new market share, new markets, or new products; otherwise, the fourth stage of decline and release won't be far behind. Profit margins tend to be at their best in this phase of maturity.

Mature companies who want to continue in business will look to diversify their product lines. They will typically be variations of an existing product line or service. For example, when we were starting our Selling Among Wolves training program, we began with an audio coaching program on cassette. This later morphed into CD, but also into a two-year, once-a-week study course conducted over lunch with fellow sales professionals and business owners. Keeping with that theme, we offered e-mail coaching and an interactive blog; then, as we matured, we offered a series of related products on the same subject.

If you look at the publishing industry, if an author has a best seller, the publisher will make sure the author releases a series of new books on related topics. They don't say, "Well, your cookbook sure was successful. I wonder how you would do writing about financial planning." The publisher of this book has been a joy to work with and, in anticipating the wide acceptance of this book, already contracted for additional works related to business development, quite possibly related to the rainforest. No matter how good your original product or service is, it won't meet the need forever, so anticipate that and develop variations and improvements on a theme to meet your customers' needs and wants.

As cash flow stabilizes in this phase of your growth, explore new avenues of income so not all your revenue comes from one stream. If you're not constantly innovating, you're not growing, and if you're not growing, you're dying. Look at 3M—the absolute glorious model of a mature business that has segments of their business in every stage of development. They invest wisely and continuously come up with new, innovative products to change the world in which we live. The sticky notes they accidentally developed with a batch of glue gone bad evolved from an innovation to growth, where every office had them, to maturity and variation where they come in all sorts of shapes and sizes, but they will one day become irrelevant and no one will use them. It will have been a nice ride, and for some people it could have been their entire business, and a good one at that, but after endless variations, it's time for a new innovation or you risk being replaced by someone else. In the rainforest and with 3M, diversity is the key to longevity.

The National Federation of Independent Business (NFIB) carried an article by Jeffrey Moses addressing this issue. In it he states, "This principle has been taken to the extreme by certain large corporations, which have diversified into a variety of industries. General Electric, for example, one of the country's oldest and largest corporations, has become a conglomerate. Its 'roots' today are in industries as diverse as airplane engines, broadcasting and consumer finance. This diversification serves to protect the company from cyclic business changes, giving it a stability that helps support future growth. While a small business could not diversify to the extent of General Electric, by putting down a variety of roots any small business can work toward creating insulation against ups and downs in its particular market segment."[8]

PHASE IV—DECLINE AND RELEASE

This phase is marked by shrinking market, lack of innovation, and declining profits. This doesn't have to mean the end of your business. It can mean as the title suggests, that you release old things and redeploy resources for something new. In the forest, the tree may die, but the species continues and the organic compounds of the dying tree are used to fuel new life. In business, perhaps the current design has become obsolete. You don't have to close down the business; just replace it with something much better.

This phase is typically marked by declining sales over a period of several years (not just an off year), the loss of a healthy bottom line due to increasing costs that outpace sales growth, or the arrival of competitors who not only gain significant market share but also take away your prime, loyal customers. If you find yourself in this mode right now, it isn't necessarily the end. Here's what you need to do:

1 Face the facts. Don't continue on in denial, blaming things on the competition, the union, the economy, and so on. Get an accurate assessment of where you are.

2 Reinvent the plan or the model. If you keep doing the same thing the same way, you will get the same result. It's time for some bold, *innovative* steps. Get help from the outside. Outside consultants do not see the same barriers you see and also have a broader experience across numerous industries that can help you.

3 Stop the leakage. Cut costs where you can. Eliminate excess. Over the years, there has probably accumulated excess in many places. Go on a hunt and eliminate it. There are also some things that can be eliminated temporarily.

4 Lean hard into the new direction. Some trees in the rainforest, when faced with drought, will drop their leaves (eliminate excess) for a season and then produce a tree full of flowers to attract new customers (marketing). When times are tough, cut back on any number of things, but double up your efforts on attracting and maintaining good customers.

The journey through each phase varies by industry and by business. You need to rightly discern the phase your business is in now so you can plan appropriately and establish realistic goals for the future. Bear in mind that your business may be in one phase and your industry in another. Your job is to be aware of these distinct phases so you can plant in the springtime and reap in the fall.

THE GRAND CYCLE

This is another one that can really trip you up if you're not paying attention. Each phase in the cycle can last for hundreds of years and have lasted for thousands. When they change, not only should you be aware, but you also need to be wise enough to know what to do. The first phase in the grand cycle that most historians acknowledge was referred to as the Stone Age. It was followed by the Bronze Age and then the Iron Age, each one radically redefining life at some level. But then came the industrial age, which we have all been a part of, and is now transitioning into the information age. People who don't have a stake in the industrial age are looking to the information age to make their future and stake their claim.

Phase changes in the grand cycle don't occur on a magical date. The transition may take decades or longer to fully replace the previous phase. We have been in transition for decades already, and the pace of that transition is increasing. In a metaphorical sort of way, we are back to the Stone Age because the information age runs on silicon, which comes from sand, which comes from ground-up stones. It's the new Stone Age! (Say I with a smile.) Always try to discern what season your are in, what season your business is in, what season your industry is in, what season our civilization is in, and remember: a leader is one step ahead of the crowd; a martyr is two steps ahead!

ACTION STEPS

1 What phase is your business in?

2 What phase is your industry in?

3 What phase are you in?

4 What are you doing to prepare for the next phase in your life and each part of your business?

■　■　■　■

11

THE BRAZIL NUT EFFECT
Leverage Through Strategic Relationships

Alone we can do so little; together we can do so much.[1]

HELEN KELLER

If you do not seek out allies and helpers, then you will be isolated and weak.[2]

SUN TZU

...companies should expand beyond their existing resources through licensing arrangements, strategic alliances, and supplier relationships.[3]

BUSINESSWEEK

Alliances have become an integral part of contemporary strategic thinking.[4]

FORTUNE MAGAZINE

BACK ON BARRO COLORADO ISLAND IN THE PANAMA CANAL, Dr. Fortunato pointed out a particularly attractive but subtly colored bird flying through the forest. She explained that certain bird species fly through the forest in search of a parade. They are looking for army ants marching through the forest. The reason they look for the ants is not so they can eat them. They leave that up to other predators.

They follow them to their destination because many times the ants are attacking a nest of termites or other insect that takes flight to escape the army ants. Millions of army ants on the move create some movement in the forest as everything wants to get out of the way. During the ensuing chaos, the fleeing insects become prey to a variety of birds loosely categorized as "army ant–following birds."

OPPORTUNISTIC RELATIONSHIPS

As Dr. Fortunato pointed out, they epitomize what is known as an opportunistic relationship. The birds don't create the opportunity, but they do take advantage of it. By definition, one party benefits without it being an expense to the other. So the bird benefits and the army ant isn't harmed. (There's no mention of the fleeing insect, but I'm not a big fan of insects anyway.) As it turns out, there are three main categories of these army ant–following birds. The first is quite casual, only following army ants that happen to be foraging in their territory. The second group is serious, more advanced, and knows a good thing when they see it, so they follow the army ant swarms outside their territory. If it turns out that the ants aren't foraging when the bird is hungry, they will find their own food through another means. Then lastly, there are a group of birds, professional army-ant followers as they are known, that are completely reliant on the army ants for food.

In my view, opportunistic relationships are the lowest value relationships in the rainforest that are still considered positive ones. It's one species relying on another for good fortune. Opportunistic relationships happen more by chance than by planning, though you can position yourself to capture opportunity when it comes (cash, liquidity, personnel, and the like). With opportunistic relationships you are dependent upon circumstances beyond your control, so it's harder to build your business on them, but not impossible. Keep your eyes open for them, but don't depend on them.

There are numerous ways to mimic opportunistic relationships and benefit financially. For example, your next-door neighbor is having his house foreclosed. You could take advantage of that situation by purchasing it and renting it out. After all, it's a great deal, your neighbor would rather you get the good deal than a stranger, and the bank is happy to get it off their books. That is a casual, opportunistic relationship. You might keep your eyes open for any others in your subdivision, but you make your money some other way. It's just like the time a friend called us and told us to mail him a check for $18,000 and we would own a new lot in some subdivision. We did as he suggested, and he sold it for me as promised for nearly double our investment a few months later. That was an opportunistic opportunity.

Now suppose you bought the foreclosed house next door, rented it out right way, and it was cash flowing positively right away. You might ramp up your commitment to opportunistic real estate by actively seeking foreclosures through the newspaper, banks, and other foreclosure databases. Now instead of acting on something because you see it in your neighborhood, you start looking elsewhere for the army ants (mortgage companies, banks, and so on) that are foreclosing on residential properties, and you develop a nice little side business, perhaps to pay for the kids' college education or fund your retirement. In the meantime, you keep your day job, your regular business. That's a serious opportunistic relationship in real estate.

Well, maybe you've done so well doing this part-time that you decide you're going to make all of your money in this business. So now, not only do you look for opportunities far and wide, but also this is your full-time business. That makes you a professional opportunistic businessperson in the real estate field. There's nothing wrong with that, if that works for you.

Now that you understand what the three levels look like in business, let's consider other forms of opportunistic relationships. It may be an opportunity that arises due to a special circumstance like the Olympics coming to your city. The opportunity may develop due to some other situation beyond your control, but if you can spot it, you can take advantage of it. When we had our small book publishing company, there was a best-selling financial book that was flying off the shelves of every bookstore. We bought them wholesale and packaged them with our books, and it boosted our sales. Be on the lookout for trends that could help your business even if it is technically a competitor.

A business consultant I knew placed an ad in a forum that I would never have thought to do myself. He received over two thousand responses from his $800 ad. I was surprised by the response, and it inspired me to advertise to the same list to see how that would work for me. I bought three ads to get a discount and spaced them out a bit. I was a bit like the bird that happened to see a grasshopper fly up when the army ants came by, only I never saw the army ants. My first ad resulted in over seven thousand people opting onto my free coaching e-mail. (You can too; just visit my blog at www.SellingAmongWolves.com.) The response was overwhelming for the investment we made, and each of our successive ads were for different products that all did exceptionally well. I decided to become a serious instead of a casual opportunistic operator with this source. It's not often you average a fifteen to twenty times ROI for direct-response advertising, so we bought up every available date through the end of the year and enjoyed great success with them. We chose not to go to the professional level and *only* advertise with them, which was smart because in the new year, they quit accepting direct-response advertising from anyone.

The application of the opportunistic relationship is simple. If a good opportunity comes along that works with your business model, snap it up. If it works well, be more deliberate about it. Pursue it. Develop it. Maximize the result. I would advise against going all the way and being fully dependent on it because it's never good to be fully dependent on another business to keep your business working. I have heard stories about large retailers who give some business to smaller companies and that retail account becomes a larger and larger piece of their business until they are dependent on that one account for their survival. In the process, the large retailer begins dictating what the pricing will be and what their profit margin will be. It can be an awfully unpleasant experience if their needs change and they go elsewhere. If you do find a good opportunity, seek out who or what caused it. What happy circumstance has benefited your business in the past or could benefit it in the future or has benefited a similar business to yours? Determine if it is likely to repeat. See if there is any way you can be forewarned. In our advertising good fortune, we sought to identify their profile and duplicate elsewhere.

PARASITIC RELATIONSHIPS

Dr. Fortunato told me about another type of relationship called parasitic. It's where one party benefits at the expense of another. A blood-sucking tick would be an example. It is exploitive in nature. Blood-sucking ticks prey on the vulnerable, the naïve, and the unsuspecting. They typically begin with a small, innocent request, but they don't leave, growing in their demands upon you subtly at first, then arrogantly at last until you have nothing left to give. The strangler fig is a classic example. So are some credit card companies! Did you know that if you charge $5,000 on a credit card, then cut it up and never use it again and begin paying only the 2 percent minimum payment required (until changed in 2006) at 18 percent interest, it will take you forty-six years to pay it off? That's parasitic!

The housing debacle of 2008 that ultimately took down Bear Stearns and greatly weakened our financial system preyed upon less-than-savvy people with subprime mortgages at unbelievably low rates that were only temporary in nature. It allowed folks to get into more house than they could afford, and the lenders knew it. Furthermore, income qualifications and credit qualifications were all out the window. If you could breathe and sign your name, it seemed, you could get a mortgage. Lenders competed to see who could throw the biggest saddle on you, sometimes offering to finance up to 125 percent of the home value, and even that was often times artificially inflated. Parasites sometimes get the upper hand, but nobody likes a parasite, and once they are discovered, there's quite the effort to get rid of them. Maybe that's what's happening in 2008. It can be very difficult to terminate your relationship with a parasite, so you will have to get tough with them. Don't be a parasite yourself, and don't be a victim of one either. If it's too good to be true, it's probably a trap.

SYMBIOTIC RELATIONSHIPS

The third type of relationship Dr. Fortunato told me about was the symbiotic relationship. This really caught my attention because by definition, a symbiotic relationship is where there is cooperation between two parties and they both benefit. It was just the mention of symbiosis between different bee species in the rainforest a year earlier by some other trekkers that first got me hooked on going into the rainforest. Leaf-cutter ants and their famous fungus farms are a marvel of nature and perhaps the best-known example of symbiosis.

The larger ants cut up green leaves into pieces several times their body dimension and haul them off to the nest where medium-size ants will shred them and miniature ants inoculate them with a fungus that digests the leaves, grows into a mushroomlike fungus, and, in turn, feeds the ants. These guys are farmers, and they're getting a lot of help from fungi that grow to the size of a football in their underground chambers. One leaf-cutter nest can easily have hundreds or even a thousand of these chambers all hidden from plain view, buried in an underground city ten to twenty feet below the surface and housing over a million ants. Some biologists believe that up to 15 percent of the new leaf production each year in tropical forests disappears down the nests of leaf-cutter ants.

Capuchin monkeys lap nectar from flowers in trees as part of their varied diet. In the process, they get pollen on their faces and pollinate other flowers. It's the "I'll scratch your back and you scratch mine" plan. You see it in a hundred different ways in the rainforest, and you see it a lot in business these days. Nike got together with Apple and created the iPod Nano for example. Think of them as strategic alliances that give you a strategic advantage in competitive situations. It's not a novel idea at all, as 20 percent of the revenues produced by Fortune 500 companies come from symbiotic relationships.

This is not just the domain of big corporations, however. Find a strategic partner with whom you will have synergy where the sum of the whole exceeds the sum of the parts. Examples abound, including the grocery store and the ATM machine. In one town a local restaurant and movie theater team up. The restaurant promotes the theater and the theater promotes the restaurant. Together they make a date night package, and both benefit. What relationships do you have or could you have that would enable you both to grow and to benefit? Who in your world values something you have in abundance and has the potential to carry you places you could never get to on your own? Maybe trade your wisdom or extra office space or surplus product for their influence, access, or contacts.

I know of an air conditioning company and a pest control company in my city that both emphasize environmentally friendly solutions. I suggested they team up and direct each other's customers to each other. Think about it. The air conditioning company already has the loyalty of a certain customer base. It would be far easier for them to get their symbiotic partner, the pest control people, in the door with a quote or some offer than it would be for the pest control company to get that opportunity on their own. This could be done through billing inserts in the mail, cross training with field reps, carrying each other's brochures, Web links, and the like. You can also form symbiotic relationships with your supplier and do joint advertising. Lastly you can create internal symbiosis by developing complementary lines of business and proactively helping each team.

MUTUALISTIC RELATIONSHIPS

Mutualistic relationships are symbiotic relationships where cooperation is not only beneficial but also necessary for survival. This is about high commitment where high rewards are possible. It's the automobile manufacturer and the car dealer relationship. It's the small business and the independent rep firm they hire. It's the venture capitalist and the entrepreneur. It requires more effort and constant attention, but it carries the greatest potential for rewards.

My wife thinks squirrels are rats with fur. She doesn't like them. They climb on top of our pool cage and use the swimming pool for a commode. As a result, I don't like them either! They do, however, resemble a rodent common in the Amazonian rainforest, called the agouti. They are cute little rodents that weigh up to ten pounds, with extremely sharp front teeth, and are solely responsible for reseeding the forest with Brazil nuts and ensuring the next generation of trees. For centuries, scientists were puzzled because they had been unable to successfully cultivate the Brazil nut tree, nor would the trees produce fruit in recently cleared rainforests. They would grow nice and tall (up to two hundred feet or more) and would live a long time (five hundred to eight hundred years), but they wouldn't produce any nuts.

That's when the scientists discovered just how extensive and delicate symbiosis is with the Brazil nut tree. In order for the tree to produce fruit, it needs a certain kind of bee to pollinate its flowers. That bee, in turn, requires a certain species of orchid to survive. To further complicate the scenario, male bees of that species must acquire the fragrance of this particular orchid in order to attract female bees. If the forest is damaged by clear cutting, the orchids disappear, along with the bees and the Brazil nuts. The male bees want the food from the Brazil nut tree, but the female bees insist that the male bees wear the fragrance of a particular orchid they could care less about. When it comes right down to it, however, if the bee has to choose between the orchid so he can have romance or the Brazil nut flower so he can have food, he chooses the orchid. That is why, when rainforests are cleared or damaged but the Brazil nut trees are left, the orchids disappear, and the bees leave looking for more orchids and the Brazil nut trees go unpollinated and produce no nuts.

Now here comes the agouti. Not only is the pollination of this tree so specialized, requiring one particular insect species to produce the fruit, but only one species of animal is capable of chewing through the extremely tough nut shell to disburse the seeds for new tree growth. That's right, it's the agouti. Here's the way I see it. The agouti has legs and lots of mobility but no food. The Brazil nut tree has lots of rich food in abundance but not legs and no mobility, so they strike up a deal. The tree offers the agouti all the food he can ever eat or carry away in exchange for one small favor. That favor is to carry some of the nuts a little further into the forest and bury them underground so they can germinate and continue on the species. The nuts themselves are rich in selenium, and if you cut one open, you can light a match to it and it will burn like a candle.

What is happening in that transaction is they are exchanging what they both have in abundance for what they desperately need and have little or none of. They are not using cash. This is not bartering. This is a value exchange and a very rewarding type of transaction. How much is continuation of the species worth to a Brazil nut tree? Apparently the trees are willing to share all their Brazil nuts with the agouti in abundance. How much is the food worth to the agouti? Apparently he is willing to be an indentured servant, planting nuts all over the rainforest. Of course, the agouti is burying the nuts for later consumption, but he may not live to eat that meal, or he may simply forget where he buried them all. But the key thing here, and this is essential to understand, is that they are trading excess for excess. The cost to themselves is negligible, but the benefit is huge.

In bartering, you typically fix a price on the value of your product or service and trade it for an equal value as determined by the price tag on the other product. There's nothing wrong with that practice, but it's not as good as trading value determined by the buyer (instead of by what the seller thinks the market will bear) with value. A major national business magazine asked me what I would charge for some of my customized sales training I was known for. Having recently returned from the rainforest and just getting to understand this principle, I replied, "What's money between friends? All I want is one side of a piece of paper." Needless to say, they were perplexed, so I made it nice and simple: "Trade me out a few full-page ads [which carried a price tag of $63,000 per ad], and I will help your sales team."

Now, my sales training is very good, but I typically do not charge a six-figure amount for a couple of days of training. They perceived the value of my unique training but only had to free up one side of a piece of paper in their magazine, which cost them very little. Both of us were able to transact this in a way that cost us little but benefited us greatly. Had I merely traded $10,000 or $20,000 worth of training for advertising, I would have only received a small classified ad at the back of the magazine. By trading value perception for value perception, we both got a better deal.

Think of it this way: I know of a Russian artist who paints magnificent oversized paintings of flowers in about twenty-four hours. They sell for many thousands of dollars. He can turn out hundreds of paintings a year if he chooses. Let's say there was an old man who grew rare herbs with phenomenal curative properties for rheumatoid arthritis all over his three-hundred-acre mountain ranch. For some reason, they only grew on his property, and most died away each year with the hard, cold winters.

Now let's say that artist was suffering with rheumatoid arthritis, hindering his ability to paint, and wanted those herbs to cure himself, but the only place he could get them was from the old man on the mountain. What do you think he would be willing to trade for them? Ordinarily the old man could sell his herbs in the village for a few dollars, but if he wanted to, he could trade abundance for abundance. If the old man loved fine art, they could probably strike a deal because most artists have lots of paintings in their studios waiting to be sold. They could trade excess for excess, abundance for abundance, and it would cost neither of them very much. The old man on the mountain could acquire great art for a bouquet of herbs, and the artist could be free from his rheumatoid arthritis for a painting he has in his studio he just painted yesterday. Both would walk away happy.

When you trade value for value, you are trading the value the other party places on your product or service for the value they place on their own product or service to themselves. The value they declare to you is not the value they see for them. In other words, the artist believes his painting is worth $25,000 and won't take a penny less, but if he saw that exact painting elsewhere on sale, he wouldn't pay $50 for it because he could do it himself.

Mutualism has the highest potential return simply because of the higher commitment to each other. It's not a casual happenstance relationship, but rather a very intentional relationship involving the investment of time, talent, and treasure. Create mutualistic relationships for highest value, symbiotic for good value, and opportunistic for short-term value. Whose business can you help grow that will help you grow in return?

Most alliances fail for the same reasons innovations often fail—poor leadership, poor organization, poor communication, unclear goals, misalignment of goals, poor participation, and lack of measuring results. Symbiotic and mutualistic relationships need constant care and attention because business isn't static. So many things are constantly changing from a technical perspective, personnel perspective, competitive angle, operational issues, and financial issues. The upside is that successful relationships produce higher profits, higher ROI, and greater innovation. That is why it is believed that many of the competitive battles in the marketplace of the future will be between strategic alliance groups rather than individual companies. To consider the value of this proposition, ask yourself what would happen to your company if a competitor created an alliance group with the best-in-class providers to your current customers? How vulnerable are you? Be proactive and seek out symbiotic and mutualistic relationships with which you can create a powerful defense (and offense). Keep your eyes open, and whenever it makes sense, create an opportunistic relationship and reap those benefits as well.

ACTION STEPS

1 Identify any business relationships that may provide you opportunities from time to time that will help your business and cost them nothing.

2 Identify any business relationships that have potential symbiosis. How could it work for both parties?

3 What do you have in abundance that you can trade with someone who has in abundance something you need? Do not trade price for price. Trade value.

■ ■ ■ ■

12

WEALTH SECRET #7

THE ORCHID ELEMENT
Creating Irresistibility

Customers buy for their reasons, not yours.[1]

ORVEL RAY WILSON

If you're trying to persuade people to do something,
or buy something, it seems to me you should use their
language, the language in which they think.[2]

DAVID OGILVY

People don't want to be "marketed TO"; they want to be
"communicated WITH."[3]

FLINT MCGLAUGHLIN

S WE WALKED THROUGH THE SHADOWY FOREST FLOOR WITH flashes of sunlight peeking through the treetops courtesy of the occasional breeze creating a fleeting opening, our eyes on occasion would be riveted upon a bold, bright, and stunningly beautiful orchid or flower. We would be walking along drinking in the oxygen-rich air and then *WHAM*! There it was—this stand-alone flower dangling like a temptress from a tree beckoning birds and bees alike to partake of her succulent pollen. Who could resist? I certainly don't eat pollen, but yet I found myself trekking over fallen trees and other organic matter to get close enough to capture the beauty on film so I could share its charm with others. This wasn't so much a chance occurrence as it was a carefully crafted script playing out along my pathway. I wasn't the intended audience, but ignoring its presence was like ignoring my wife's homemade southern pecan pie. There is no good reason to do that!

Dr. Fortunato explained that some of the trees we were looking at had no leaves because it was the dry season, and when resources are scarce, some trees drop all their leaves just to produce the flowers. As I mentioned earlier, she told me it was for marketing purposes. The trees had to produce flowers to attract pollinators so there would be fruit or seeds to be passed on to reproduce future generations of the same kind of tree. The lesson I got from that is when resources are scarce, you might have to cut back in many areas, but be sure to get your sales and marketing efforts out or there will be no next generation.

Noticing how compelling orchids and tropical flowers are, I was eager to get home and begin extensive research on what makes a flower the best form of marketing as opposed to a leaf or a stem or something else altogether. The first things I uncovered are what I call the seven constants that are true of all orchids. The seven constants are aptly true in marketing and should always be taken into consideration when planning a marketing campaign.

SEVEN CONSTANTS

1. Color

Color interacts with color perception. Hummingbirds are attracted to red and orange, while other pollinators see ultraviolet colors on flowers that humans cannot see. It is well established that color has a psychological impact on people. Although the results may vary, the generalizations are helpful to know. Have you ever been to a blue and green fast-food chain? Neither have I. Fast-food chains are usually warm colors like orange and yellow because that stimulates hunger and cheerfulness. Blue, pink, and purple tend to be calming. Green is fresh and natural feeling. Color sends a message about you and what you are offering.

2. Fragrance

This interacts with the sense of smell. There are some flowers that smell like rotting flesh. While they are not what you would choose for your kitchen table, these flowers attract flies that aren't interested in all the nice-smelling flowers. Fragrance as a form of advertising tends to be limited to products we associate with a particular smell, but sometimes smell is used to attract customers. Retailers have been known to prepare fresh popcorn just inside the store to draw you into the store. I am convinced some restaurants deliberately take the air from the kitchen and pump it out onto the street to attract customers as well! The fragrance communicates a message. It might be dinnertime or it could be bedtime, but it always has a message.

3. Shape

This interacts with the recipient. Some orchids have a shape certain pollinators find very attractive. Bee orchids, for instance, look and smell just like a female bee. Male bees are attracted to the plants because the flower looks like a receptive female, and during a frustrating attempt at mating with the flower, the male bee will become the unwitting carrier of pollen, which it will duly deposit on its next amorous flight of fancy. An interesting thing about shape that is often overlooked is that you can attract a lot of attention to your product or service by introducing a design concept with an unusual shape. In a world of squares, a round object definitely catches your attention. My good friend and amazing graphic artist Mark Herron taught me, "When the world is zigging, it's time to zag." Shape, color, and fragrance conspire together to send a clear, compelling message about who they are and what they have to offer.

4. Size

The size of the orchid to some extent determines the size of the pollinator. Small orchids keep out many would-be pollinators as a way of further refining their target audience. Size is a common consideration for advertising, as evidenced in full-page ads vs. classified ads, billboard ads vs. bus stop ads, Jumbotrons, and the Goodyear blimp. The size, shape, color, and fragrance not only apply to the ad but also to your product, which is also an ad for your product. Choosing the size of a book, for example, is part of the marketing of that same book.

5. Timing

Not only do you want to aim at your target audience, but you also want to do it at the right time. One species of flowering plant I saw in the highlands of Panama opens at night to attract bats. No sense in opening shop during the day when the bats are sleeping. No sense advertising snow shovels in April or Christmas cards at Easter. More to the point, though, is knowing when your target market is most likely to be receptive to your service. If you offer credit repair services, find out from credit reporting agencies who is struggling with credit issues.

6. Location

This provides the context. It is the target audience's environment. In the rainforest, flowers are positioned in the best proximity for their intended customer. Capuchin monkeys never have to leave the tree to eat. The flowers best suited for them are not on the ground but up in their habitat. Coincidence? I think not. But then I am a believer in intelligent design. What environment does your customer frequent? Target that environment. If you're selling entry-level housing, target apartment dwellers. How many McDonald's restaurants do you see in swanky, high-end parts of town? I've never seen one there. They tend to be where their most likely customers are. Drive through a poor part of town and notice the billboard advertising and what it promotes and whom it targets. Much of it is exploitive in nature, but it makes the point that the marketers are targeting the location from which comes most of their business.

7. Medium

The old saying "The medium is the message" was coined by Marshall McLuhan and means that the medium itself becomes embedded in and inseparable from the message, resulting in a symbiotic relationship where the medium itself actually impacts and directs how the message is perceived. If someone leaves a black-and-white flyer on your windshield in the parking lot, you attach one meaning to the message and quite a different meaning if you see the ad on television during the nightly news. In the rainforest, the tree is the medium, and that conveys its own message to the pollinator.

Every species of orchid is designed to attract specific pollinators. They are very clear on who they are, who their market is, where there market is, and when best to attract them. You never see a bee orchid trying to attract a hummingbird. They are wired for their market, built especially to succeed within that market, and they use exactly the right traits or constants in the right combination to appeal to their base while being willing to repel others. While the strategic combinations are endless and very informative, they all send the message to folks in business: marketing is a nonnegotiable for long-term growth and sustainability.

Scientists recently discovered a rare palm in Madagascar that literally flowers itself to death while ensuring the preservation of the species. According to Kew Royal Botanical Gardens in London, at the end of the life cycle of this palm, "a pyramid of hundreds of tiny white flowers spring from the top of the tree. The flowers drip with nectar, announcing the palm's swan song to swarms of birds and insects. Once pollinated, the tree sends all remaining nutrients to its flowers as they develop into fruit. Then it collapses and dies."[4] It reinforces the message that marketing is an investment every business must make.

SEVEN NATURAL LAWS OF MARKETING

After endless hours of studying and synthesizing the marketing lessons revealed by tropical flowers like the orchid, I was able to boil it down to what I call the Seven Natural Laws of Marketing. Before sharing my findings with anyone, I wanted to test it in my own business. At the time of this discovery, my income was largely derived from sales training and consulting as well as speaking at conferences. Our Web site was more of a brochure, and the store was generating only hundreds of dollars per month in product sales.

The first thing we did was change our Web site so that visitors (pollinators) would not only check us out and perhaps buy something but also recommend us to their friends. Our revenues doubled the first month and again the second month, and our daily rate continued to double in the third month. We encountered significant technical challenges, so our site was offline for half the month, but our volume in half a month roughly matched the entire previous month. We were only beginning to get our brains around the concepts and how to implement them in the information distribution side of our business.

One of the things we learned was that your site doesn't have to be cute or fancy or awesome. It needs to be *effective*. What makes for an effective Web site depends on the purpose of the site. A number of folks were less than impressed with the graphics of our site, but did I lose any sleep over that? Not a chance! For the first time ever, our online sales were rapidly accelerating, and it didn't matter if it was pretty! But we went further, much further. After returning for another rainforest trip and seeing first-hand how the rainforest economy thrives and how much emphasis is put on marketing, we ramped up our commitment to marketing using the seven natural laws. The next three months we were doing twice as much revenue on a daily basis as we had been doing in an entire month. It wasn't long before we were generating a six-figure revenue number in a quarterly sales cycle. I realize as impressive as this may be, much more is possible. I have chosen, however, to apply these lessons to the endowment for the business school, and we are currently experiencing a seven-figure revenue number just about every week on average. For a small foundation almost no one had ever heard of one year earlier, that is not small potatoes! Without further ado, let me introduce the seven natural laws.

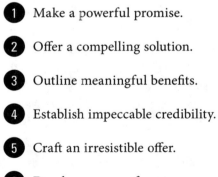

1 Make a powerful promise.

2 Offer a compelling solution.

3 Outline meaningful benefits.

4 Establish impeccable credibility.

5 Craft an irresistible offer.

6 Develop a sense of urgency.

7 Give a clarion call to action.

LAW #1—MAKE A POWERFUL PROMISE

Target your audience.

Orchids make a bold promise with their design, color, and scent, but their promise is always targeted to a specific audience, as demonstrated by the bee orchid. Your expertise, more than anything else, defines your target market. It allows you to speak from your position of authority, expertise, and confidence. When you speak from your position of strength, your target audience will recognize your authority and are more likely to respond. Get real clear on who your target audience is, and remember that you may have several.

Headlines are the ad for the ad.

The orchid flower is the ad for the pollen inside. Give your headline top priority when designing an ad. According to branding and advertising legend David Ogilvy, "Five times as many people read the headline than do the body copy in a sales message. This means that unless your headline actually helps sell what you've got to offer, you'll have wasted 90 percent of your time, money and energy."[5] I once read an account by the well-respected, highly paid Jay Abraham, who told a story about a client of his years ago in the precious metals business. They were running an ad in a national print publication and generating about $50,000 worth of business from each ad. They wanted to know "how high is high?" so they hired Jay to see if he could improve the ad.

When he read the ad, he thought it was good and only changed the headline. It had originally read, "2/3RDS BANK FINANCING ON GOLD AND SILVER." When he changed just the headline to, "If Gold Is Selling for $300 an Ounce, Send Us Just $100 an Ounce, and We'll Buy You All The Gold You Want," it outpulled every other headline by no less than 300 percent![6] Imagine tripling your response rate because you used the right headline. The way to find out is to test, test, test. Little things like surrounding your headline with quotation marks can increase readership by over 25 percent, because it implies something important is being said. Nevertheless, you need to see if that holds true with your target market. Things like ALL CAPS are actually harder to read and gets lower response rates.

Color is a form of headline.

It's bold, striking, and commands your attention: "I have what you want!" What is the boldest, truthful claim you can substantiate? When we were actively seeking new sales training clients, our headline read, "How Our Clients Reliably and Consistently Grow Sales and Increase Profits, Despite Ruthless Competitors Who Focus on Price, Commoditize the Industry, and Way Over Promise!"

The headline appeals to self-interest.

Orchids appeal to their customer's highest needs and/or wants. People choose wants over needs. Find the "want" behind the "need." They may need a certain car for their job, but what they really may want is their job.

Use curiosity to attract interest.

"See my petals?" We use titles like the 7 Wealth Secrets of the Rainforest for our original CD series or Selling Among Wolves—Without Joining the Pack! to garner interest in our teaching materials. You might also try something like, "The Top Ten Foods You Should Never Eat!" It seems people just have to know what those are. Use that to attract curiosity, but be sure to deliver on your promise.

Speak their language.

Orchids are designed in such a way as to attract their perfect customer. They know what their customers are after, and they give it to them. The slipper orchid lures a thirsty insect with a promise of a drink from its pouch. In drinking the water, the insect slips inside the orchid, and the only way out is through a tight passage, laden with pollen. What are your prospects thirsty for? Appeal to that.

Lead with the pain.

Many hungry insects are in search of rotting flesh to feast on. Some orchids smell like rotting flesh to attract those insects. Your customer is far more conscious of their pain than they are of your solution. What pain do your prospects have? Appeal to their area of pain—"Are you hungry?" What is the biggest pain or fear your prospects have? You can lead with that.

Lead with a testimonial.

Some orchids resemble a dove poised and ready for flight, mimicking a happy customer just leaving. Endorsements work.

Give something FREE.

Orchids offer free food, free drink, and so on to attract customers. What's your offer? Consider offering a free report, a complimentary sample, an MP3 download, or a bonus newsletter subscription.

The orchid makes design and scent work together.

Make your headlines and graphics work together. Use upper and lower case for headlines. You can even tell a story in the headline.

LAW #2—OFFER A COMPELLING SOLUTION

This is where you capture the heart. Appeal to the right brain. Speak the language that connects with their desire: "I have what you are looking for—fresh pollen." State your solution in clear, concise, and immediately identifiable terms. When I was actively seeking corporate sales training opportunities, our Web site read, "We come alongside your organization to transform your team into a highly productive, well-disciplined, market-leading, profit-producing team of professionals who love what they do because they are winning!" It was clear, concise, and very compelling. It was also true!

The right side of the brain loves analogies and is highly imaginative, artistic, and creative, but your communications should not leave the left side unaddressed. Your marketing should appeal to the emotional right side and the logical left side. Use your medium to create the "want to" first, which occurs in the right side of the brain. Then make it a "need to" by providing the logical, rational justification for the investment you are asking them to make. If you cover both the right-brain "wants" and the left-brain "needs," your message will be received on both the cognitive and affective levels. We will deal with left-brain specifics when we get to the fourth law, but as a quick recap, here are the seven right-brain (HI SPEED) strategies to include in your marketing message:

H EIGHT: BIG PICTURE PERSPECTIVE; SPEAKS TO HIGHER PURPOSE

I LLUSTRATION: REVEALS FUNCTIONALITY; PUTS NEW INFORMATION IN FAMILIAR TERMS

S TORY: PUTS A MULTIPLIER INTO THE VALUE OR PERCEIVED VALUE

P ASSION: AMPLIFIES, ANIMATES, AUTHENTICATES PERCEIVED VALUE

E MPATHY: IDENTIFY WITH PROSPECT; MEET THEM ALONG THE CONTINUUM

E XPERIENCE: FIND A WAY TO LET THE PROSPECT SEE INSIDE

D ESIGN: THE FIRST MULTIPLIER OF VALUE. "LETTERS MEAN NOTHING UNLESS ARRANGED IN THE RIGHT ORDER. BRING MATERIAL COMPONENTS TOGETHER IN THE RIGHT ORDER AND SOMETHING VALU-ABLE MAY SPRING FORTH. THE VALUE ISN'T IN THE MATTER; IT'S IN THE DESIGN."[7]

LAW # 3—OUTLINE MEANINGFUL BENEFITS

People don't want your product. They want the product of your product. What it will do for them.

—Michael Q. Pink

The message of the bee orchid is very meaningful to the bee. It is, "If you try my pollen, you will be well fed and smell nice, which will attract a mate, make you very happy, and give you many sons." The lesson here is to state the benefits back to your prospects in terms that are meaningful to them. The benefits do not typically include how big your building is or how long you've been in business. Those things speak to credibility issues perhaps, but the benefits must answer the question, "What's in it for me?" Will they be healthier, happier, richer, thinner, or smarter? Make sure your ad copy focuses on the advantage they will enjoy because they did business with you.

Knowledge releases information and speaks of the solution, but knowledge merely informs. It is power but only in reserve. To generate action, understanding must take place. Revealing the benefits is what creates understanding, and understanding is what motivates action. It inspires transformation. It creates the "Aha!" moment where you suddenly "get it." Understanding motivates because it appeals to the right side of the brain. When listing the benefits you bring to the table, list them in descending priority to your target market's known highest wants and needs. Sometimes the benefit of most importance is the secondary benefit. If you are selling a weight-loss supplement, the primary benefit is weight loss, but the secondary benefit may be improved self-esteem, better health, or social acceptance.

Wisdom, on the other hand, reveals justification, provides confirmation, and speaks of intellectual validation. Wisdom decides. It lives in the left-brain world. It buttons down all the justification and makes perfect sense. Nobody really wants a fiber-optic Internet connection. They do want something reliable, operating at high speed that can handle any load, day or night, regardless of who else may be online at that given moment. The fiber-optic cable buried beneath the ground to protect from storms or accidental downing is part of the wisdom because it explains the "how." The rest of the logic may well be the security of knowing you won't be knocked offline and no one else can penetrate the firewall.

LAW #4—ESTABLISH IMPECCABLE CREDIBILITY

Credibility can be defined as, "capable of being believed; believable; worthy of belief or confidence; trustworthy."[8] Credibility earns you the right to be heard and gives the person you're speaking to justification to listen. This is nothing less than the Law of the Brand that John Muratori outlines masterfully in his book, *Rich Church Poor Church*. John explains, "Businesspeople will recognize the brand as a company name or product name. Corporations spend millions of dollars defining themselves through their names, symbols and identities, then even more keeping that brand name in front of the public. Your name is your brand and you should give priority to establishing a good name for yourself. Most people will never get to know you intimately, so your character is only known by the name and reputation that precedes you. A good name carries with it a high perceived value. If you have a reputation of honesty and integrity, you'll find more doors opened to you, more acceptance into circles of influence and more resources given to you. If you have a reputation of getting the job done, of cutting costs or producing wealth, you are worth more in compensation to an employer or client."[9] John cites the wisdom of Solomon for his foundational premise: "A good name is rather to be chosen than great riches, and loving favor rather than silver and gold."[10]

"You can smell it from where you are! A million other bees can't be wrong!"

How can you establish credibility? What references do you have? What have you accomplished on behalf of clients? What is your training? How successful have you been? These are all things potential clients or customers want to know. Nobody wants to be a guinea pig. Who has gone on before them and been successful with your product or service? Let your customers know there is a stampede headed in your direction. If it's early on with a new product, share previous successes you have had.

Define your specific advantage.

People now know they want the kind of product you are offering. What they need to know is why they should get it from you. What uniquely qualifies you to serve them? If the sale is made that they need a high-speed Internet connection, the next decision is who they should get it from. You must help the prospect see what differentiates you from the competition. Orchids are very good at this, with over twenty thousand species attesting to this fact.

Credibility is essential.

If you have it, use it. If you're new, lean on the credible track record of your suppliers, skilled personnel, or proven system. In my case, though I have a very credible background in sales and business, for this book I am relying on the credibility of something far more well known with a much longer track record of unbroken success—the rainforest. Where appropriate, attach your product, your company, or your person to something of even higher credibility or acceptance with your target market.

Offer an iron-clad guarantee.

The stronger the guarantee, the lower the resistance on the part of the prospect. Thirty days is better than seven days. A year is better than a month. We found with selling our audio coaching program that increasing the strength of our guarantee not only increased our conversion rates on the Web site, but it also almost completely eliminated returns of any kind. Here's how our guarantee reads: "Tenfold Return—Guaranteed—Or Your Money Back! What I will promise you is this: If you don't experience a tenfold return on your investment in the next twelve months, then this would have not been right for you, and we invite you to return it for a full, no-hassle return. Where else are you going to get a tenfold return—guaranteed? I'll even pay the postage!" How can you validate your claims? Offer a strong guarantee that projects confidence in your product or service.

You must satisfy the left brain, the portion that is logical, analytical, loves order and sequence, and enjoys math, problem solving, decision making, and formal language. As you address this side of the brain, keep these six (LINEAR) concepts in mind:

L OGIC ORIENTED: BRING THE HEART TO WISDOM

I NFORMATION BASED: WHAT QUALIFIES YOU? SHOW FACTS, FIGURES, AND PICTURES

N UMBER JUSTIFIED: ROI, TOTAL COST OF OWNERSHIP, COMPARISON

E VIDENCE LADEN: INDEPENDENT REPORTS, PROVEN TRACK RECORD

A NALYTICAL IN APPROACH: THIRD-PARTY ANALYSIS

R EFERENCES: TESTIMONIALS DISPERSED LIBERALLY

A powerful promise backed up with an iron-clad guarantee:

- Increases value perception

- Separates you from the others

- Communicates confidence in your product, service, or abilities

- Lowers resistance to your offer

- Increases conversion rates

In face-to-face situations, credibility allows you to move more quickly into fruitful discussions about their needs and your solutions without having to justify everything you say along the way. It creates a more relaxed atmosphere, making it easier for you to ask for the go-ahead to whatever the next step is. As helpful as references are, they really just prove that you've been successful helping other folks, which earns you the right to jointly discover if you can do the same for them. I said "discover" because in a face-to-face setting, you shouldn't assume you know the solution that is best for them before diagnosing the situation first. Visit my Web site www.SellingAmongWolves.com if you would like to learn about a questioning strategy Moses employed before invading Canaan that has helped numerous clients of mine secure tens of thousands of dollars of extra sales in a very short time.

Resist the urge to impress. Choose to ask good questions and listen. Go a little deeper with the questions, and take a sincere interest in the answers. All the while you are building personal credibility with the prospect, and, when coupled with the corporate credibility already established, you are well on your way to a healthy business relationship.

LAW #5—CRAFT AN IRRESISTIBLE OFFER

Many orchids are so designed to look like either an aggressor of the pollinator or its sexual partner. In the case of the bee orchids, for instance, male bees are attracted to the plants because the flower looks like a receptive female bee.

Put together a special offer that creates extra incentive to make that purchase. Orchids use every stimulant possible to make themselves irresistible to their target market. We experimented with our information products, offering both the downloadable form and the physical CDs. We found a substantial number of people would rather have the download but would enjoy the physical copy to give as a gift, so we offered the CDs at our regular price, and to make it extra attractive, we offered the downloadable version FREE. Then we reversed it and offered the downloadable version for a 20 percent reduced price (from the physical product price) and made it extra attractive by offering the physical product for just those few dollars extra. That way they were getting the teaching for their iPod and, for a few bucks extra, getting a $100 gift for a friend or loved one.

Some orchids adopt the lure technique and have long stems, the tips of which bear their flowers; these can dance effectively in the breeze and look amazingly like butterflies. Of course, other butterflies find this irresistible either because they want to make new friends or they want to challenge them for the territory. Either way, the sale is made and the pollination takes place.

The slipper orchid lures the insect with a promise of a drink from its pouch. Consider offering something FREE: "No charge. Try a free sample." What can you offer from your abundance as a way of introducing folks to your company? (We use a daily coaching e-mail, an MP3, and a thirty-minute consultation.)

Work with your symbiotic partners to create a special promotional offer. Promotions that tie into themes like "back to school" or " graduation" or seasonal promotions like Christmas or Valentine's Day work very well regardless of whether or not your product actually has anything to do with the season.

When reading your ad, your customers are going to give you three seconds to make the sale. Craft an offer with strong appeal to your target market. Be specific with your offer. Don't try to be all things to all prospects. Do you know what to say in those three seconds? Use this chapter to help you figure it out. J. D. Moore of Marketing Comet knows exactly what to say in those three seconds, and when he used this headline, the readers found it absolutely irresistible: "Give Me Just 1/2 Hour Of Your Time And I'll Show You 3–4 Ways To Triple Your Business—It Costs You Nothing....I'll Even Pay For The Phone Call." The intended response was a sample coaching consultation, and his conversion rate increased by nearly 300 percent![11] Go and do likewise.

LAW #6—DEVELOP A SENSE OF URGENCY

A lot of marketers lose credibility at this stage because the reason that's offered for urgency is bogus, and anyone with half a brain can tell it. If they will lie to you about that, what else will they lie to you about? Having said that, there are often legitimate limitations that create urgency.

Limited time

"Better get some while we're in season." In the rainforest, flowers and fruit typically come in seasons. There is a limited time that they can offer their wares. It is 100 percent legitimate. Similarly, there are certain offers that come with built-in time limitations, such as certain tax deductions. Work with established and accepted seasons that relate to your product. Having a New Year's Day sale is a legitimate limited-time event. The more logical you can make the time limitation, the better. Where appropriate, remind people of genuine time limitations, but avoid even the appearance of "bogus."

Limited quantity (scarcity)

"Once the pollen is gone, it's gone." Genuine scarcity creates demand. We discontinued our audiocassette products in favor of CDs. That allowed us to offer the last 413 sets we had in stock for a special price. Once they were gone, that opportunity would never be available again. To be clear, never use artificial scarcity. You lose credibility with your customers and in the mirror if you ever take a long, hard look.

Limited offer

"This pricing available for the first fifty or first five hundred orders." We did a promotion where we ordered five hundred books that were to be used as a giveaway for the first five hundred orders. It was an authentic offer, and we had a response very close to our estimated demand. Early-bird registration is another example of providing a special benefit to a limited group.

Offer bonus for immediate action

"Orders received by June 15 will receive our bonus CD, *Profiles of Success*." Again, you have the right to create incentive for your customers to buy. We have done numerous offers where we offered bonus items for a quick response. To us, it was worth the extra bonus to close the sales quickly.

Whatever the course of action, clearly define why taking action now is imperative. Never use artificial limitations. The limitations you describe must be believable, justifiable, and reasonable! Brian Clark from Copyblogger.com says, "Never pressure people to PUSH them into purchasing. Instead, use pressure to PREVENT them from procrastinating."[12] I have always said I would rather draw you into something than push you into it. My goal is to make you willing and joyful to take the next step, not pressured and coerced! It's more about drawing you in than pushing you in.

The *Marketing Experiments* journal wrote extensively on the topic of creating urgency. They found that "while using urgency is a powerful promotional tool, it should not be used indiscriminately or without forethought.... Urgency should be genuine and not simply created as a promotional gimmick. The growing sophistication of online audiences means that many people can and will recognize 'manufactured urgency.' Even the legitimate use of an urgent message will still be recognized as a promotional tactic. So if your message is not completely genuine and honest, you run a very real risk of losing the respect and loyalty of some of your readers. The use of urgency on an offer page can be a very powerful tool, but is not something you can do all the time. If you do, you will lose credibility."[13]

LAW #7—GIVE A CLARION CALL TO ACTION

This is about warmly, confidently, and very, very clearly inviting the guest on your Web page or magazine ad to take the next step. That next step should be clearly defined so there is no question whether they are supposed to fill out a form, call your office, or just say a prayer! Here are some simple guidelines:

 Make it logical. The next step should make sense. "Call this number now for your free..." "Click here for your free report..." "Return this card to claim your..."

 Make it reasonable. I've seen a lot of companies make the mistake of asking the prospect to take a bigger step than they're comfortable with. Recently we offered a $1,500 ninety-day mentoring program for Internet marketing of brick-and-mortar businesses. We didn't deem it reasonable to ask readers to make that size of a purchase based on just the e-mail. We knew some would act, but most would want more interaction. So instead of asking for the sale, we invited them to a free teleseminar with a choice of multiple dates where we would discuss the content at length and answer questions. Hundreds of people were comfortable taking that step, and the tele-seminar was crammed with useful information of high value. After providing that value, we invited them to sign up for the program, but our response from the first teleseminar was still less than hoped for. So we added an intermediate step where they could schedule a personal thirty-minute consulta-tion with our Internet guru to make sure this was right *for them*. That was the key and resulted in our highest grossing promotion to date. Finding the right next step is critical, and it must make sense to the prospect.

③ Make it simple. Using the teleseminar example, we made sure that it was so easy to attend this tele-seminar a caveman could figure it out his first time! Clearly and simply define what the next step is for the customer. You should say what you want them to do, how you want them to do it, and when you want them to do it.

④ Make it natural. It should just feel like everything has been addressed so that it's only natural to proceed!

⑤ Make it multiple choice. On our Internet marketing, even though we want folks to click here and order, there are a fair number who prefer to read about it online and then call a toll-free number to order. Give them that flexibility.

Applying these laws to marketing pieces both in print and in long-form landing pages on the Internet has significantly and dramatically increased the response rate not only for our company but also for other clients. Remember that sometimes one small change can make a big difference, so be sure to test multiple versions of your promotion. Sometimes the defining difference is the headline, while other times it's the size of step you are asking them to take. The bigger the step, the stronger your risk reversal (guarantee) needs to be. Although there is very much a scientific aspect to marketing, it is also an art. If you would like assistance with your Internet marketing efforts, feel free to contact us at 877.254.3047 or e-mail us at admin@rainforestinstitute .com.

ACTION STEPS

1 Write out a compelling, powerful promise for your product or service.

2 What is your solution, described in twenty-five words or less?

3 List the three top benefits clients can expect to experience if they purchase your product or service.

4 How will you establish impeccable credibility?

5 What can you add to make your offer irresistible?

6 How will you help customers understand the urgency?

7 What will your call to action be?

CONCLUSION

YOU HAVE TAKEN THE FIRST STEP BY READING THIS BOOK. Now be sure to act upon at least the three most important points you read. Be deliberate. Be decisive. Be purposeful. I want to hear from you and see what you applied and how that worked out for you. We might just use your story in the sequel!

One way you can stay in touch is to join one of our coaching e-mail groups. You can check them out at www.SellingAmongWolves.com or www.SecretsoftheRainforest.com.

I would also like to send you a free audio download of one of my talks on this subject just to say thank you for reading this book and for introducing yourself. Just e-mail us at admin@RainforestStrategy.com to request your free download.

If you want to really heighten the value of your experience, be sure to join me and some of my highly successful CEO friends who have built remarkable enterprises and applied some or all of these principles in their businesses. They have agreed to be part of a small mentoring group that meets in the rainforest at the nicest resort we can find close to a rainforest. For more information, contact our office at 877.254.3047.

RAINFOREST COMPLIANT

As another service to our corporate clients, we have trained consultants who work with me to help your business become *rainforest compliant*. In that process we work with you to increase productivity and improve profitability by doing one or more of the following:

 Help you develop a strategic vision that becomes part of the company dialogue.

 Do a fungigation analysis looking for profit opportunities currently being missed.

3 Perform a pest analysis and put in place practices to help your team master the No Pest Zone and skyrocket your productivity.

4 Initiate a pathogen analysis to look for dangerous pathogens threatening your organization. A bad apple really can spoil the whole bunch! We will identify internal threats and help you deal with them appropriately.

5 Develop an updated business process for your company (including sales) and get the entire team clear on goals, objectives, benchmarks, and performance metrics.

6 Strategize to identify possible opportunistic, symbiotic, and mutualistic relationships to grow your business.

7 Develop and craft irresistible marketing messages, including writing copy for long-form Internet landing page ads.

To request a confidential thirty-minute consulting interview to see if this makes sense for your organization, go to www.RainforestInstitute.com and request a complimentary consultation. If you prefer, you can call our office at 877.254.3047.

NOTES

CHAPTER 1
THE EPIPHANY

1. BrainyQuote.com, "John Milton Quotes," http://www
.brainyquote.com/quotes/quotes/j/johnmilton400414.html
(accessed June 12, 2008).

2. Tachi Kiuchi and Bill Shireman, *What We Learned in the
Rainforest: Business Lessons from Nature* (San Francisco, CA:
Berrett-Koehler Publishers, 2002), back cover.

3. SavetheRainforest.org, "Facts About the Rainforest," http://
www.savetherainforest.org/savetherainforest_007.htm (accessed
June 12, 2008).

4. Ibid.

5. Ibid.

6. 1 Kings 4:33–34, KJ21

7. 1 Kings 10:14, KJ21

8. 1 Kings 10:15, KJ21

9. Romans 1:20

CHAPTER 2
BREAKING THE CODE

1. Giga Quotes, "George Dana Boardman American
Clergyman," http://www.giga-usa.com/quotes/authors/george_
dana_boardman_2_a001.htm (accessed May 19, 2008).

2. ThinkExist.com, "Anton Chekhov Quotes," http://thinkexist
.com/quotation/knowledge_is_of_no_value_unless_you_put_it_
into/221938.html (accessed May 19, 2008).

3. World of Quotes, "James Allen Quotes," http://www
.worldofquotes.com/author/James-Allen/1/index.html (accessed
May 20, 2008).

4. William F. Laurance, "Gaia's Lungs—Forests Help in Keeping
Carbon Dioxide Out of Atmosphere," *Natural History*, March
1999, http://findarticles.com/p/articles/mi_m1134/is_2_108/ai_
54032999 (accessed June 13, 2008).

5. Wikipedia.com, "Critical Mass (Sociodynamics)," http://
en.wikipedia.org/wiki/Critical_mass_%28sociodynamics%29
(accessed June 13, 2008).

CHAPTER 3
SPONTANEOUS WEALTH

1. ThinkExist.com, "Jamie Paolinetti Quotes," http://thinkexist
.com/quotation/limitations_live_only_in_our_minds-but_if_
we_use/254292.html (accessed May 20, 2008).

2. QuoteDB.com, "Brian Tracy," http://www.quotedb.com/
quotes/2322 (accessed May 20, 2008).

3. World of Quotes, "Benjamin Franklin Quotes," http://www
.worldofquotes.com/author/Benjamin-Franklin/4/index.html
(accessed May 20, 2008).

4. David G. Myers, "Wealth, Well-being, and the New American
Dream," http://www.davidmyers.org/Brix?pageID=49 (accessed
May 20, 2008).

5. Daniel Gilbert, *Stumbling on Happiness* (n.p.: Vintage
Canada, 2007).

6. BrainyQuote.com, "Thomas Jefferson Quotes," http://www
.brainyquote.com/quotes/quotes/t/q143405.html (accessed May
20, 2008).

7. Mississippi State University, "Quotes From Famous
Scientists," http://www.msstate.edu/org/sacs/quotes.html
(accessed May 20, 2008).

8. Lock Haven University of Pennsylvania. "Science Quotes: Beauty in Science," http://www.lhup.edu/~dsimanek/sciquote .htm (accessed May 20, 2008).

9. LeaderNetwork.org, "Leader of the Month for February 2006: Charlie 'Tremendous' Jones," http://www.leadernetwork.org/ charlie_jones_february_06.htm (accessed June 13, 2008).

10. Quotations Page, "Quotations by Author: Thomas A. Edison," http://www.quotationspage.com/quotes/Thomas_A._ Edison/ (accessed May 20, 2008).

CHAPTER 4
WEALTH SECRET #1: THE FUNGUS FACTOR

1. As quoted by Global Change of University of Michigan, "The Tropical Rainforest," November 2, 2005, http://www .globalchange.umich.edu/globalchange1/current/lectures/kling/ rainforest/rainforest.html (accessed May 20, 2008).

2. The American Institute of Stress, "Job Stress," http://www .stress.org/job.htm?AIS=b8b2dadd521368bf6c75ef603b4e197f (accessed June 13, 2008).

3. SaveYourWorld.com, "Reasons to Save the Rainforest," http:// store.saveyourworld.com/Save-Your-Rainforest-s/34 .htm (accessed June 13, 2008); Vegetarian-Restaurants.net, "Eco-Commerce: The New Paradigm," http://www.vegetarian -restaurants.net/Amazon-Herbs/Tropical-Rainforests-Eco -Commerce.htm (accessed June 13, 2008); Answers.com, "Tropical Rainforest," http://www.answers.com/topic/tropical -rainforest-ecology?cat=technology (accessed June 13, 2008).

4. BrainyQuote.com, "Golda Meir Quotes," http://www .brainyquote.com/quotes/authors/g/golda_meir.html (accessed May 20, 2008).

5. Xenophon A. Koufteros, Mark A. Vonderembse, and William J. Doll, "How to Cut Manufacturing Throughput Time," https://umdrive.memphis.edu/g-cscm/www/ctr5/ manufacturingthroughputtime.pdf (accessed May 20, 2008).

6. Kiuchi and Shireman, *What We Learned in the Rainforest*, 33.

7. ThinkExist.com, "William Arthur Ward Quotes," http://thinkexist.com/quotation/flatter_me-and_i_may_not_believe_you-criticize_me/15189.html (accessed May 20, 2008).

8. Scott Elliott, "The Power of Encouragement," *Dayton Daily News*, December 29, 2006, http://www.daytondailynews.com/blogs/content/shared-gen/blogs/dayton/education/entries/2006/12/29/the_power_of_en.html (accessed June 13, 2008).

9. University of Queensland, "Stimulated Brain Cells Won't Self Destruct," February 7, 2008, http://www.sciencealert.com.au/news/20080702-16865-2.html (accessed May 21, 2008).

10. Memory Disorder Project at Rutgers University, "Use It Or Lose It: the Key to Healthy Brain Aging," Memory Loss and the Brain, Summer 2004, http://www.memorylossonline.com/use_it_or_lose_it.htm (accessed May 21, 2008).

11. University Libraries, Virginia Polytechnic Institute and State University, "What's Been Said About Learning," http://learning.lib.vt.edu/aboutlearn.html (accessed June 13, 2008).

12. Psychology.org, Explorations in Learning & Instruction: The Theory Into Practice Database, "Experiential Learning (C. Rogers)," http://tip.psychology.org/rogers.html (accessed May 21, 2008).

13. Seneca, *Letters to Lucilius* (excerpts), Letter 76, http://praxeology.net/seneca.htm (accessed June 13, 2008).

14. Plato, *The Republic*, translated by Benjamin Jowett, http://classics.mit.edu/Plato/republic.html (accessed May 21, 2008).

15. Kiuchi and Shireman, *What We Learned in the Rainforest*, 26–28.

16. *Corporate Real Estate Leader*, November/December 2006.

17. Adam Smith, *An Inquiry into the Nature and Causes of the Wealth of Nations* (Chicago, IL: University of Chicago Press, 1977).

18. Ibid.

19. Mary Cann, "Study Shows Diversity Is an Advantage," *Epoch Times*, February 6, 2006, http://en.epochtimes.com/news/6-2-6/37840.html (accessed May 21, 2008).

20. Ibid.

21. Ibid.

22. Cheryl McGaughey, "Dry As a Bone," EconEdLink.org, May 17, 2005, http://www.econedlink.org/lessons/index.cfm?lesson=EM536&page=teacher (accessed May 21, 2008).

CHAPTER 5
PRACTICE ABUNDANCE

1. See John 10:10.

2. Quote DB, "Albert Einstein Quotes," http://www.quotedb.com/quotes/1348 (accessed May 21, 2008).

3. "Quotes For Strength," http://www.motivatingquotes.com/strength.htm (accessed May 21, 2008).

4. WorldMysteries.com, "Nuclear Energy," http://www.world-mysteries.com/sci_9.htm (accessed June 13, 2008).

5. Numbers 13:33, KJ21

6. Numbers 14:9, KJ21

7. Betty Edwards, *Drawing on the Right Side of the Brain* (New York: Tarcher, 1989).

8. Daniel H. Pink, *A Whole New Mind* (New York: Berkley Publishing Group, 2006), 102.

9. Donald A. Norman, *Things That Make Us Smart* (New York: Perseus Books, 1993). 129–130.

10. Pink, *A Whole New Mind*, 106, referencing Stephen Denning, *The Springboard: How Storytelling Ignites Action in Knowledge-Era Organizations* (Woburn, MA: Butterworth-Heinemann, 2001), xvii.

11. Ralph Kerle, "Creativity and Business," *Business/Higher Education Round Table 23*, March 2006, 5, viewed at http://www.bhert.com/documents/B-HERTNEWS23.pdf (accessed June 14, 2008).

12. Mark Victor Hansen and Robert Allen, *The One Minute Millionaire* (n.p.: Harmony, 2000).

CHAPTER 6
WEALTH SECRET #2: GROW TOWARD THE LIGHT

1. Proverbs 29:18, KJ21

2. Kris Vallotton, "The Power of a Vision," http://www.ibethel.org/FEATURES/JOURNAL/15/THE-POWER-OF-A-VISION/KRIS-VALLOTTON (accessed June 14, 2008).

3. Matt Bertz, "League Leaders: Don't Give Up on the NBA Just Yet—Here Are 7.5 Reasons We're Sticking With It Another Year," *Men's Fitness*, November 2005, http://findarticles.com/p/articles/mi_m1608/is_9_21/ai_n15732087 (accessed June 14, 2008).

4. *Forrest Gump*, directed by Robert Zimeckis, DVD (Hollywood, CA: Paramount Pictures, 2004).

5. Ibid.

6. "Vision" Definition, http://www.yourdictionary.com/vision (accessed May 22, 2008).

7. GE.com, "Past Leaders: John F. Welch Jr.," http://www.ge.com/company/history/bios/john_welch.html (accessed June 14, 2008).

8. "Quotes to Inspire You: Orison Swett Marden," http://www.cybernation.com/victory/quotations/authors/quotes_marden_orisonswett.html (accessed May 22, 2008).

9. PersonalGrowth101.com, "Inspirational and Motivational Quotes," http://www.personalgrowth101.com/PG101quotes.html (accessed May 23, 2008).

10. WorldofQuotes.com, "James Allen Quotes," http://www
.worldofquotes.com/author/James-Allen/1/index.html (accessed
May 23, 2008).

11. MotivationToday.com, "Motivational Quotes and
Quotations," http://www.motivationtoday.com/motivational_
quotes/motivational_quotes_and_quotations.php (accessed May
23, 2008).

12. Proverbs 29:18, NKJV

13. Matthew E. May and Kevin Roberts, *The Elegant Solution:
Toyota's Formula for Mastering Innovation* (n.p.: Free Press,
2006), 109.

14. Reported in *Business Reform Magazine*, Joe Johnson,
publisher.

15. See Proverbs 24:16.

16. Quote by Oliver Goldsmith, as seen at http://annesbattle
togoal.blogspot.com/2007/05/its-not-whether-you-get-knocked
-down.html (accessed June 14, 2008).

CHAPTER 7
WEALTH SECRET #3: ENTER THE "NO PEST ZONE"

1. QuoteLand.com, "M Scott Peck Quotes," http://www.quote
land.com/author.asp?AUTHOR_ID=463 (accessed May 23,
2008).

2. ThinkExist.com, "John Lubbock Quotes," http://thinkexist
.com/quotation/in_truth-people_can_generally_make_time_
for_what/181286.html (accessed May 23, 2008).

3. Time Management Central, "Time Management Quotes,"
http://www.time-management-central.net/time-management
-quotes-2.html (accessed May 23, 2008).

4. Cynthia L. Sagers and Phyllis D. Coley, "Benefits and Costs
of Defense in a Neotropical Shrub," Department of Biology,
University of Utah, Salt Lake City, Utah.

5. Claudia Wallis and Sonja Steptoe, "Help! I've Lost My Focus," *TIME*, January 8, 2006, http://www.time.com/time/magazine/article/0,9171,1147136,00.html?promoid=rss_top (accessed May 23, 2008).

6. Ibid.

7. Ibid.

8. MailOnline.com , "We're Not Skivers, Say Workers Based at Home," May 18, 2007, http://www.dailymail.co.uk/news/article-455698/Were-skivers-say-workers-based-home.html (accessed June 16, 2008).

9. Wallis and Steptoe, "Help! I've Lost My Focus."

10. Phyllis D. Coley and Thomas A. Kursar, "Anti-Herbivore Defenses of Young Tropical Leaves: Physiological Constraints and Ecological Tradeoffs," in *Tropical Forest Plant Ecophysiology* (New York: Chapman and Hall, 1996), 305–336.

CHAPTER 8
THE PATHOGEN PROBLEM

1. GetMotivation.com, "The Motivational Speaker's Hall of Fame: Dr. Maxwell Maltz," http://www.getmotivation.com/maxwell_maltz.htm (accessed June 16, 2008).

2. BrainyQuote.com, "Maxwell Maltz Quotes," http://www.brainyquote.com/quotes/authors/m/maxwell_maltz.html (accessed May 23, 2008).

3. MentalHealthAmerica.org, "Factsheet: Gaining a Competitive Edge Through Mental Health: The Business Case for Employers," March 12, 2007, http://www.nmha.org/go/gaining-a-competitive-edge-through-mental-health-the-business-case-for-employers (accessed June 16, 2008).

4. As reported in Pennsylvania Health Care Cost Containment Council, "PHC4 FYI: The Costs of Depression in the Workplace," http://www.phc4.org/reports/FYI/fyi22.htm (accessed June 16, 2008).

5. Partnership for Workplace Mental Health, "A Mentally Healthy Workforce—It's Good for Business," http://www.work placementalhealth.org/pdf/POPartnershipBrochure05.pdf (accessed June 16, 2008).

6. Kate Mulligan, "Data Show Employers How Health Affects Bottom Line," *Psychiatric News* 37, no. 10 (May 17, 2002): 17, viewed at http://pn.psychiatryonline.org/cgi/content/full/37/10/17 (accessed June 16, 2008).

7. Martin Sipkoff, "Depression is Prevalent and Pernicious, Costing Employers Billions Each Year," *Depression in the Workplace*, Spring 2006, 4, viewed at http://www.managed caremag.com/supplements/0603_depression_in_workplace/ DepressionInWorkplace_Spr2006.pdf (accessed June 16, 2008).

8. *The Lion King*, directed by Roger Allers and Rob Minkoff, DVD (n.p.: Walt Disney Studios, 1994).

CHAPTER 9
WEALTH SECRET #4: THE PHOTOSYNTHESIS OF IDEAS

1. Memorable-Quotes.com, "Memorable Quotes and Quotations From Theodore Roosevelt," http://www.memorable-quotes.com/ theodore+roosevelt,a589.html (accessed May 23, 2008).

2. Goal-Setting-Guide.com, "Goals," http://www.goal-setting -guide.com/quote-goal.html (accessed May 23, 2008).

3. Author interview with Wes Cantrell.

4. BrainyQuote.com, "Zig Ziglar Quotes," http://www.brainy quote.com/quotes/quotes/z/zigziglar380875.html (accessed June 16, 2008).

5. BrainyQuote.com, "Peter Drucker Quotes," http://www.brainy quote.com/quotes/authors/p/peter_drucker.html (accessed May 23, 2008).

6. Author interview with Wes Cantrell.

7. ThinkExist.com, "Earl Nightingale Quotes," http://thinkexist
.com/quotation/your_problem_is_to_bridge_the_gap_which_
exists/256149.html (accessed May 23, 2008).

8. ThinkExist.com, "Alan Lakein Quotes," http://thinkexist
.com/quotation/planning_is_bringing_the_future_into_the_
present/194902.html (accessed May 23, 2008).

9. BrainyQuote.com, "Khalil Gibran Quotes," http://www
.brainyquote.com/quotes/quotes/k/kahlilgibr100753.html
(accessed May 23, 2008).

10. BrainyQupte.com, "Thomas Carlyle Quotes," http://www
.brainyquote.com/quotes/quotes/t/q122761.html (accessed May
23, 2008).

11. QuoteWorld.com, "Thomas Alva Edison Quotes," http://
www.quoteworld.org/quotes/3998 (accessed May 23, 2008).

12. Michael and Brenda Pink, *Psalm 91—The Ultimate Shield*
(Nashville, TN: Nelson Bibles, 2003).

CHAPTER 10
WEALTH SECRET #5: THE STRANGLER FIG PHENOMENON

1. Ecclesiastes 3:1–2, KJ21

2. Psalm 1:3, KJ21

3. Kiuchi and Shireman, *What We Learned in the Rainforest.*

4. Egbert Giles Leigh Jr. with Christian Zieglar, photographer, *A
Magic Web* (New York: Oxford University Press, 2002).

5. Richard Foster and Sarah Kaplan, *Creative Destruction* (n.p.:
Financial Times Prentice Hall, 2001).

6. Ibid.

7. Associated Press, "Bark Beetle Infestation Is Killing Forests
in the West," February 2, 2008, http://www.dailybulletin.com/
ci_8150279 (accessed June 16, 2008).

8. Jeffrey Moses, "The Four Potential Stages of Business Growth, Part II," National Federation of Independent Business, http://www.nfib.com/object/2873311.html (accessed May 27, 2008).

CHAPTER 11
WEALTH SECRET #6: THE BRAZIL NUT EFFECT

1. ThinkExist.com, "Helen Keller Quotes," http://thinkexist.com/quotation/alone_we_can_do_so_little-together_we_can_do_so/144236.html (accessed May 27, 2008).

2. Sun Tzu, *The Art of War* (n.p.: Shambhala, 2005).

3. As quoted by Corporate-partnering.com, "Strategic Alliances and Partnering Quotes," http://www.corporate-partnering.com/info/strategic-alliances-and-partnerings-quotes.htm (accessed May 27, 2008).

4. Ibid.

CHAPTER 12
WEALTH SECRET #7: THE ORCHID ELEMENT

1. Museum Marketing Tips, "Motivational Quotes: Marketing and Advertising," http://www.museummarketingtips.com/quotes/quotes_ac.html (accessed May 27, 2008).

2. BrainyQuote.com, "David Ogilvy Quotes," http://www.brainyquote.com/quotes/authors/d/david_ogilvy.html (accessed May 27, 2008).

3. Museum Marketing Tips, "Motivational Quotes: Marketing and Advertising," http://www.museummarketingtips.com/quotes/quotes_ac.html (accessed May 27, 2008).

4. Adam Hinterthuer, "Palm's Magnificent Death May Save Its Life," *Scientific American*, January 21, 2008, http://www.sciam.com/podcast/episode.cfm?id=8EB3680B-01E4-07BD-4965D13D81296E85 (accessed June 17, 2008).

5. Debbie Jenkins, "Killer Business Headline Templates," Bookshaker.com, http://lean.bookshaker.com/champions/27 .html (accessed June 17, 2008).

6. Jay Abraham, *Money Making Secrets of Marketing Genius Jay Abraham and Other Marketing Wizards* (n.p.: Abraham Publishing Group, 2002).

7. Kiuchi and Shireman, *What We Learned in the Rainforest*.

8. "Credibility," Dictionary.com, Dictionary.com Unabridged (v 1.1), Random House, Inc., http://dictionary.reference.com/ browse/credibility (accessed: June 17, 2008).

9. John Muratori, *Rich Church Poor Church* (n.p.: Gatekeeper Publishing, 2007).

10. Proverbs 22:1, KJ21

11. J. D. Moore, "Give Me Just 1/2 Hour Of Your Time And I'll Show You 3–4 Ways To Triple Your Business—It Costs You Nothing…Heck, I'll Even Pay For The Phone Call," Small Business Marketing Coach, http://www.marketingcometcoach .com/small_business_marketing_coaching/index.php (accessed June 17, 2008).

12. Brian Clark, "The Smart Way to Create a Sense of Urgency," Copyblogger.com, http://www.copyblogger.com/the-smart-way -to-create-a-sense-of-urgency/ (accessed June 17, 2008).

13. Cliff, "Sense of Urgency," The Marketing Experiments Journal, November 29, 2006, http://www.marketing experimentsblog.com/internet-marketing-strategy/sense-of -urgency-29-06.php (accessed May 27, 2008).

Want to ELIMINATE Waste, CAPTURE Lost Opportunities, MAXIMIZE the Reach of Your Resources, HARNESS the Power of Symbiosis, FEND OFF the Pests, and GET MORE Done... *Without Breaking a Sweat?*

We will come alongside you and your team for about three days to clarify the vision, sharpen the focus, and lay out a *road map to take your business where you've always wanted it to go.* Here's where we will focus our expertise:

- **Vision:** We'll see if *the vision is driving decision and energizing the team.* If not, we'll show you how to get there.

- **Waste:** Typically, 80 percent of the things you focus on bring only 20 percent of your revenue. We'll help you find lost profit opportunities.

- **Pests and pathogens:** Nothing robs productivity like pests and pathogens. *We'll help you set up "No Pest Zones" so productivity can soar!*

- **Process:** Whether it's the sales process or business process, we will *help you design the best process for maximum results.*

- **Cycles:** We will give you strategies to guide you and your business safely through the innovation, growth, maturity, and release phases.

- **Symbiosis:** We will brainstorm with your team to help you *leverage what you have in excess for what you need most.*

- **Marketing:** We will look at ways to *create irresistibility in your marketing efforts* through the grid of the orchid element.

If you are an entrepreneur, business owner, or senior executive who wants to discover if this is right for you, call us at 877.254.3047 for a thirty-minute exploratory conversation, or e-mail us at admin@RainforestStrategy.com.

ARE YOU RAINFOREST COMPLIANT?
WWW.RAINFORESTSTRATEGY.COM

Note: If you are a business consultant interested in helping other businesses thrive like a rainforest, e-mail us at admin@RainforestStrategy.com.

■   ■   ■   ■

SOMETIMES YOU HAVE TO GET AWAY TO GET AHEAD

The Gamboa Rainforest Lodge was built along the Chagris River in 2000 with spacious modern rooms according to the highest hotel standards.

Come away for three days of...

Strategic business workshops conducted both in the rainforest and in the comfort of a world-class rainforest resort. Start your day off with an early morning coffee on your private balcony listening to the haunting sounds of howler monkeys echoing across the Chagris River as exotic birds greet the morning with song. Then catch the boat down the Panama Canal and across Lake Gatun to the Smithsonian's world headquarters for tropical research on the remote island of Barro Colorado.

Walk through the rainforest...

Past 40-foot-wide tree trunks under the shade of a lush canopy with monkeys and anteaters going about their day. Be prepared for an outdoor teaching experience in the most vibrant, living business model you've ever seen with symbiosis played out in front of you in many forms. Back at the lodge, I will be teaching and conducting workshops and integration sessions with other content specialists where we practically apply rainforest strategies to transform your business. This will be a rare opportunity to connect with other business leaders and build lasting relationships. You will leave with your mind full of ideas, your body relaxed, and your soul at peace. Your business will never be the same! Visit www.RainforestStrategy.com or call 877.254.3047 for details.

Want to stay longer?

Visit the cool mountains, the Caribbean coast, and the Pearl Islands in the Pacific and find out what makes this a top retirement destination for Americans.

FREE NEWSLETTERS
TO HELP EMPOWER YOUR LIFE

Why subscribe today?

☐ **DELIVERED DIRECTLY TO YOU.** All you have to do is open your inbox and read.

☐ **EXCLUSIVE CONTENT.** We cover the news overlooked by the mainstream press.

☐ **STAY CURRENT.** Find the latest court rulings, revivals, and cultural trends.

☐ **UPDATE OTHERS.** Easy to forward to friends and family with the click of your mouse.

CHOOSE THE E-NEWSLETTER THAT INTERESTS YOU MOST:

- Christian news
- Daily devotionals
- Spiritual empowerment
- And much, much more

SIGN UP AT: **http://freenewsletters.charismamag.com**

8178